Sponsor's Preface

For 250 years, the Royal Academy of Arts Summer Exhibition has set the stage for both established and emerging artists to contribute to this wonderfully unique, challenging and uplifting showcase of contemporary art.

Our association with the Exhibition has spanned more than a decade and we are honoured to play a role in its enduring success. As the world's largest open-submission exhibition, it provides such a unique opportunity for artists from all walks of life to be associated with this world-leading cultural spectacle.

In this remarkable anniversary year, the founding principles of the Summer Exhibition remain clear to see. Visitors to the Exhibition will experience an extraordinary array of works, which, under the curatorial stewardship of Grayson Perry, reaches the furthest corners of the RA's galleries and spreads further still onto the streets of London's West End in a fitting celebration of 'art made now'.

We hope everyone who experiences this year's selection of works will share our enthusiasm for this truly unique display of artistic endeavour.

Abdallah Nauphal
Chief Executive Officer

Sponsored by

Part of ➤ BNY MELLON

Stephen Cox
Prof Sir Tony Cragg CBE
Gus Cummins
Richard Deacon CBE
Tacita Dean OBE
Spencer de Grey CBE
Anne Desmet
Kenneth Draper
Tracey Emin CBE
Prof Stephen Farthing
Gilbert & George
Sir Antony Gormley OBE
* Piers Gough CBE
Nigel Hall
Thomas Heatherwick CBE
Gary Hume
Louisa Hutton OBE
Timothy Hyman
Bill Jacklin
Vanessa Jackson
Neil Jeffries
Prof Chantal Joffe
Isaac Julien CBE
Sir Anish Kapoor CBE
Michael Landy
* Christopher Le Brun PRA
Sir Richard Long CBE
Jock McFadyen
* Prof David Mach
Prof Ian McKeever
John Maine
Lisa Milroy
Prof Dhruva Mistry CBE
Mali Morris
Prof Farshid Moussavi

David Nash OBE
Mike Nelson
* Prof Humphrey Ocean
Hughie O'Donoghue
* Prof Chris Orr MBE
* Cornelia Parker OBE
Eric Parry
* Grayson Perry CBE
Prof Cathie Pilkington
Dr Barbara Rae CBE
Fiona Rae
Peter Randall-Page
Prof Ian Ritchie
Michael Rooney
Eva Rothschild
Rebecca Salter
Jenny Saville
Sean Scully
Tim Shaw
* Conrad Shawcross
Yinka Shonibare MBE
Bob and Roberta Smith OBE
Alan Stanton OBE
* Emma Stibbon
Wolfgang Tillmans
Rebecca Warren
Gillian Wearing OBE
Prof Alison Wilding
Chris Wilkinson
Jane and Louise Wilson
Richard Wilson
Bill Woodrow

* *Hanging Committee 2018*

Awards and Prizes

The Royal Academy of Arts Charles Wollaston Award
£25,000 to be awarded by a panel of judges appointed by the President
and Council for the most distinguished work in the exhibition.

The Jack Goldhill Award for Sculpture
£10,000 for a sculpture.

The Sunny Dupree Family Award for a Woman Artist
£4,000 for a painting or sculpture.

The London Original Print Fair Prize
£2,500 for a print in any medium.

The Hugh Casson Drawing Prize
£5,000 for an original work on paper in any medium, where the
emphasis is clearly on drawing.

The British Institution Awards
The British Institution Fund was established to promote excellence in
the arts through the awarding of prizes to students. Work is assessed
across a comprehensive range of creative disciplines from painting
to architecture. Two prizes of £5,000 and £3,000 will be awarded this
year by the trustees.

The Rose Award for Photography
£1,000 for a photograph or series of photographs.

Turkishceramics Grand Award for Architecture
£10,000 awarded to the most outstanding work of architecture.

The Arts Club Award
£2,500 awarded to an artist aged 35 or under for a work in any medium
except architecture.

How to Buy a Summer Exhibition Artwork

If you would like to purchase or have a query about an artwork in the Summer Exhibition, please visit our Art Sales Desk outside the galleries. You can also browse and buy artworks online at roy.ac/Explore.

The artists or exhibitors ('the exhibitors') are the sellers of the artworks and we take a commission on sales (30% of the net price plus VAT), which primarily helps to fund the RA Schools, together with our programme of exhibitions, education and debate.

All the prices in the list are inclusive of VAT, where applicable, and our commission.

When you place an order, we take a deposit of 30% of the list price from you for our commission. Then we notify the exhibitor that you would like to buy his/her artwork and he/she then contacts you to take the remaining payment and arrange delivery or collection of the artwork.

If you are buying a work on display, the exhibitor will send you a removal order so that you can collect it at the end of the show.

If you are buying an unframed print or a sculpture from an edition, the arrangements for delivery or collection are made between you and the exhibitor.

For unframed prints, the packing costs are usually included in the price (unless you or the exhibitor live outside the UK), but if you are buying a sculpture from an edition, you should expect to pay an additional charge for delivery.

Exhibitors usually respond in two or three weeks, but occasionally take longer. If you do not hear from the exhibitor within a few weeks, please contact 020 7300 5683 or email summerexhibition@royalacademy.org.uk

Red dots
If you buy an exhibited work, we will place a red dot against the catalogue number to indicate the sale. If you buy a print or sculpture from an edition, we will place a dot on the glass or plinth.

Terms and conditions of an Offer to Purchase

When you tell us you want to buy an artwork and pay us your deposit, this is your 'Offer to Purchase' the artwork.

The Offer to Purchase is registered with the artist who should, on receipt of the notification containing the offer to purchase, inform the purchaser that the offer is accepted on the condition that the work remains at the Royal Academy until after the Exhibition closes on 19 August 2018. In the unlikely event that the Artist does not proceed with the sale the Royal Academy will refund the deposit.

The Royal Academy will provide the artist with the purchaser's name and contact details. The RA will not have any liability to any person in respect of any incorrect information provided to it by the purchaser or the artist. All arrangements for payment of the balance, collection, or delivery of the artwork are made between the artist and the purchaser. If the purchaser resides outside the UK they must bear the transportation and importation costs. A VAT registered artist is required to provide the purchaser with a VAT invoice.

The purchaser may collect the exhibited artwork from the Royal Academy on production of the signed removal order between Saturday 25 August and Friday 14 September 2018, Monday to Friday between 8am and 4pm, and on Saturdays between 9am and 4pm. Collection cannot be made on Sundays or on bank holidays.

Under the Copyright, Designs and Patents Act 1988, it is the rule that, in the absence of any agreement to the contrary, copyright in a work of art belongs to the artist, or his or her heirs and assigns.

Please note that the resale of any work of art may incur a resale royalty to be paid to the artist in accordance with the Artist's Resale Right Regulations. (The work will need to be by a living artist and resell for over 1,000 euros.)

Entering work to the Summer Exhibition 2019

If you would like to enter works to the Summer Exhibition 2019, please visit our website at roy.ac/submit, where you will find all the information you need.

Summer Exhibition Committee 2018

Main Galleries	
Wohl Central Hall	Grayson Perry CBE RA
III	Grayson Perry CBE RA
IV	Prof Humphrey Ocean RA
V	Prof David Mach RA
VI	Piers Gough CBE RA
VII	Prof Phyllida Barlow CBE RA
VIII	Cornelia Parker OBE RA & Grayson Perry CBE RA
IX	Conrad Shawcross RA
Lecture Room	Allen Jones RA & Tom Phillips CBE RA
Sackler Galleries	Prof Chris Orr MBE RA & Emma Stibbon RA
The McAulay Gallery	Grayson Perry CBE RA

Plan of the Galleries

The McAulay Gallery (Burlington Gardens, ground floor)

The McAulay Gallery

Weston Bridge

↑

From Piccadilly entrance

Sackler Wing of Galleries (Burlington House, second floor)

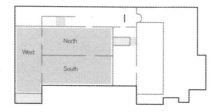

Main Galleries (Burlington House, first floor)

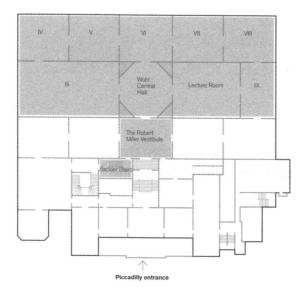

Browse and buy from the Summer Exhibition online

Browse all the works again online, share your favourites or enjoy one of our handpicked selections.

You can also purchase many of the works online. Visit us at **roy.ac/Explore**

Catalogue

The Annenberg Courtyard & Staircase

1 SYMPHONY FOR A BELOVED DAUGHTER 2018 NFS
metal and fabric
Sir Anish Kapoor RA

2 UNTITLED (PUBLIC SCULPTURE FOR NFS
A REDUNDANT SPACE)
sleeping bag, concrete and rubble
Mike Nelson RA

The Robert Miller Vestibule

3 BLUE WATER	£84,000
oil on tarpaulin	
Hughie O'Donoghue RA	
4 LE CINEMA FLEURIS: FIN	£32,000
oil on shaped board with brass rod projections	
Anthony Green RA	

Wohl
Central Hall

---

5 YOGINI – COBRA II £15,500
pencil on paper
Stephen Cox RA

---

6 NATHAN £800
watercolour
Barrington

---

7 POPPIES I: ANTHONY GAZING, MARY DREAMING £19,000
oil on shaped board
Anthony Green RA

---

8 THOUGHT LONDON £4,000
oil on metal
Neil Jeffries RA

---

9 SLEEPING CHILD £4,250
pastel and charcoal
James Butler RA

---

10 PEGGY £150
acrylic
Les Deacon

---

11 ROOFS 'MARBLE ARCH' PL28 8BG £1,200
pencil
Trevor Dannatt RA

---

12 CARD GAME WITH WHISKY £2,500
pencil
Oscar Farmer

---

13 DOWNFALL £225
c–type print
Mark Edwards
(edition of 25 at £155)

14 TAMAITI O TE HUTT £3,800
pen on tapa cloth
Jennifer Summers

15 UNTITLED £180
ink
Roy

16 REFLECTIONS IN THE ARTIST'S SPECTACLES £15,000
AND THE YELLOW CHAIR
oil on shaped board with supporting brass rods
Anthony Green RA

17 PLEASE DON'T TALK TO ME ABOUT ART £3,350
acrylic on board
Magda Archer

18 FIELD OF DREAMS £15,500
mixed media
Kenneth Draper RA

19 FLYING FOOTY £102,000
acrylic and mixed media on collaged canvas
Frank Bowling RA

20 34 WIGGLY EYES FOR M £900
archival pigment print
Agnieszka Szczotka
(edition of 34 at £650)

21 IN BETWEEN THE ISLANDS £4,800
acrylic
Jenny Wheatley

22 TEAR OF A SEAHORSE V NFS
oil
Elfia Bell-Salter

23 THE SWING £6,000
oil
Max Renneisen

24 IN THE PUB £7,200
oil
Avi Lehrer

25 GEORGE FREDERICK'S FINAL STRAW £380
acrylic
Roger Dobson

26 COTTAGE BY THE SEA CORNWALL £4,000
acrylic
Leonard McComb RA

27 PLATEAU £1,850
acrylic
Donna Gray

28 LOVE AT FIRST SIGHT £6,000
colour pencil on wood panel
Fipsi Seilern

29 NOSTALGIA ISN'T WHAT IT USED TO BE! £10,780
oil
Frederick Cuming RA

30 WE COULD USE A LITTLE BIT OF THAT GOOD £1,450
OLD GLOBAL WARMING
oil on linen
Lisa Rigg

31 THE ACADEMICIAN £3,150
oil on board
Timothy Hyman RA

32 RINSE RELAX REVIVE £780
c-type print
Camilla Bliss
(edition of 100 at £680)

33 CLEANSING OF THE POOR £2,500
oil
Michael Alan-Kidd

34 A NEW ADMISSION NFS
acrylic on board
David Beales

35 A TALE OF FLOTSAM £4,500
gouache and tempera on paper
Mick Rooney RA

36 A MOMENT OF CONTEMPLATION £1,250
oil
Sonya Howie

37 CORRECTIONS, THE HIGH LINE #64 £850
oil
Louise Langgaard

38 FOR EAD/MY UNKNOWN GRANDMOTHER £8,000
oil on board
Susan Wilson

39 UNTITLED £400
acrylic on paper
Kim

40 YELLOW TULIPS £15,000
watercolour
Leonard McComb RA

41 MR BALL MACHINE, HIS SON AND NEW £225
STEPMOTHER (WHO HAS WEIGHT ISSUES)
c-type print
Patrick Dalton
(edition of 151 at £75)

42 PANEL FOR ASCENSION £2,250
gouache on paper
John Maine RA

43 THOUGHTS OF ALMERIA £525
performance photography
Léonie Cronin
(edition of 20 at £460)

44 DYING TO GROW UP ROUND MY NECK £260
OF THE WOODS
inkjet print
Hayden Kays
(edition of 50 at £150)

45 UNDER THE CHEESEGRATER £630
[LEADENHALL STREET]
pencil
Timothy Hyman RA

46 GOD FACE APPROACHING JELLY FISH £1,200
oil
Peter White

47 WELSH COTTAGE £8,000
oil
Leonard McComb RA

48 UNTITLED, 2016 £2,250
pen and ink on paper
Bryan Kneale RA

49 ROYAL VALKYRIE NFS
hand-made woollen crochet, felt appliqués, ornaments,
fabrics, inflatable, power supply unit and steel cables
Joana Vasconcelos

50 PIAZZA DEL GESÙ NAPLES £5,000
oil on board
Ken Howard RA

51 LEFT RIGHT AND CENTRE £3,000
PEOPLE ARE WORRIED
sign writers' paint on wood panel
Bob and Roberta Smith RA

52 SCHOOL RUN MUM £375
acrylic, pen, foraged lichen and gold leaf on canvas
Georgina Wedderburn

53 WALLPAPER WALK NFS
collage, liquid gold leaf and acrylic ink
Beth Fraser

54 AFTER TACITUS C.100AD £48,000
oil
Tom Phillips RA

55 DOUBLE BILL £5,500
oil on flax
Dickon Drury

56 PITCH V £2,000
oil
Vanessa Jackson RA

57 SNOW WHITE WITH COLOURS FAIRER PAINTED NFS
oil
Fiona Rae RA

58 GIRL IN THE BLACK DRESS £10,000
acrylic
John Wragg RA

59 THE STONES OF VENICE SAN CRISTOFERO £45,000
acrylic
Joe Tilson RA

60 A LITTLE TRUMP £400
acrylic on paper
Katy Wix

61 WILD FLOWERS FROM THE BANK, LLWYNHIR £7,000
oil
Diana Armfield RA

62 YOU BETTER NOT GO ALONE £4,500
oil
David Remfry RA

63 MICROPARTICLES MOVING WESTWARDS £16,800
acrylic
Anthony Whishaw RA

64 OI OI £5,480
acrylic on panel
Stewart Geddes

65 THE GIRLS £750
acrylic
Bridget Harrison-Jeive

66 HALF & HALF ART £240
knitted acrylic
Russell Davies & Ben Terrett

67 THE ALLOTMENTS, NO: 12 £1,500
oil
Rob Reed

68 THE FALL £5,000
oil
Bryan Kelly

69 BIG ATLAS £50,400
acrylic on linen
Paul Huxley RA

70 BIRDSTORM £21,600
acrylic collage on canvas
Anthony Whishaw RA

71 SOTTERLEY LAKE £1,500

pastel

Cornelia Fitzroy

72 HERD £1,800

gouache

Sophie Wake

73 DUNGENESS MOONRISE £14,200

oil

Frederick Cuming RA

74 ROOM 3 A GALLERY OF AFRICAN AMERICAN £7,500
HISTORY: WASHINGTON DC

acrylic

Stephen Farthing RA

75 STILL TIME – UNSOCIABLE MEDIA £1,500

oil

Jacqueline Taylor

76 UMBRELLA CROSSING V £52,500

oil

Bill Jacklin RA

77 SUNRISE £6,500

acrylic

Lucy Williams

78 IN SYNC £18,000

oil

David Remfry RA

79 UNTITLED AK09 £30,000

mixed media on linen

Rebecca Salter RA

80 THE PARTY £4,200

oil

Heather Nevay

81 THE WAT'RY GLASS £21,600

oil

Fiona Rae RA

82 WINDOW £800
oil
Natasha Zavialov

83 ROYAL PROGRESS £3,850
gouache and tempera on paper
Mick Rooney RA

84 MAGIC SPELLS FOR SALE £200
screenprint
Dario Illari
(edition of 125 at £125)

85 BLACK CHAIR £3,000
oil, paper and graphite on wood
Anne Rothenstein

86 LUNCHTIME £2,000
oil
Sophie O'Leary

87 ALL FALL DOWN (FOR KARL LTONY, OLD PALS) £144,000
acrylic and mixed media on collaged canvas
Frank Bowling RA

88 NOPE 001 £950
acrylic gouache on board
Oddly Head

89 MRS MARGARET NEAVE NFS
oil
Gloria Neave

90 STUDIO SHELVES 2 £15,500
oil
Anthony Eyton RA

91 MERTON'S HOMAGE TO HOCKNEY £800
oil on board
Kate Wilson

92 THE VENETIAN DRESS NFS
oil on linen
The late Bernard Dunstan RA

93 ANTHRO EARTH £3,000
felt
Jess Warby

94 OUR NEIGHBOUR OVER THE FOOTBRIDGE, LLWYNHIR £10,000
oil
Diana Armfield RA

95 GONG SHOWER £3,900
oil on linen
Andy Harper

96 SPAGHETTI GIRLS £600
acrylic
Angela O'Connell

97 HARVEST HOME £3,900
oil
Laurence Udall

98 A GOTHIC TALE £20,000
oil
Machiko Edmondson

99 RYE HARBOUR ENTRY STORM £44,000
oil
Frederick Cuming RA

100 SELF – REALIZATION £1,950
oil on board
Carole Griffin

101 PUSSY APPEAL £1,950
acrylic
Alan Fears

102 ME 005 £895
acrylic gouache on board
Oddly Head

103 THROWING A BOOT AT THE PRESIDENT *
oil on linen
Stephen Chambers RA

Refer to sales desk.

104 PICTURES BY THE SEA £4,000
tempera on paper
David Tindle RA

105 AFTER W. H. DAVIES £58,000
oil
Tom Phillips RA

106 LIQUID GOLD £960
oil
Amanda Ansell

107 CAROLINE £7,000
oil
The late Bernard Dunstan RA

108 GUS & ELLA £2,600
analogue photograph on inkjet print
Keith Bernstein
(edition of 50 at £2,600)

109 HEAD OF A DOG £850
oil
Patricia Beach

110 BRITISH ARTISTS SERIES #1 £350
knitted wool
Rod Melvin

111 EYES AS BIG AS PLATES Prints from the edition
 # LÍSA (ICELAND) available for sale
c-type print
Karoline Hjorth & Riitta Ikonen
(edition of 7 at £2,800)

112 GARDENER'S WORLD – SUMMER £8,500
oil
Olwyn Bowey RA

113 IT'S THE PHONE OR ME £1,800
oil and acrylic on board
Caroline Lovett

114 GIRMA £9,000
oil
Catherine Chambers

115 PAINT SPILL £68,000
inkjet print
Wolfgang Tillmans RA

116 NO TITLE NFS
oil
Lale Karayaka

117 JE T'AIME MOI NON PLUS £200
marker pen on rubber gloves
Wilma Johnson

118 ANCIENT AND MODERN DOUBLE PORTRAITS £3,950
OF GIUSEPPE MARASCO AND MIKE QUIRKE
EACH PAINTS THE OTHER
egg tempera and gold leaf on board
Giuseppe Marasco & Mike Quirke

119 INTERIOR WITH TWO FIGURES £3,000
oil, paper and graphite on wood
Anne Rothenstein

120 EVE, HER FATHER AND A PASSING SHADOW £6,500
OF HER MOTHER
acrylic on gesso board
David Tindle RA

121 MORE BEAUTIFUL SUNFLOWERS £1,550
chalk
Diana Armfield RA

122 ARTWALKS 139 BELGRADE £1,900
giclée print
Milena Zevu
(edition of 30 at £1,600)

123 AFRICAN BARBER SHOP SIGN NFS
oil
Rose Wylie RA

124 BRIXTON GARDEN £18,350
oil
Anthony Eyton RA

125 NIGHT YOUTH INTERIOR £3,000
acrylic
Piers Alsop

126 ITALIAN HAT £2,350
oil
Emrys Williams

127 BRADLEY'S TEA HUT EPPING FOREST £7,890
acrylic
Martin Barrall

128 EYES AS BIG AS SAUCERS £1,400
acrylic on aluminium panel
Matilda Harrison

129 RESTING £2,000
conté crayon
The late Bernard Dunstan RA

130 THE BRISTOL 2 LITRE ENGINE £17,500
free machine embroidery
Julie Heaton

131 MOAB £3,500
oil
Jasmine Hatami

132 STUDIO SHELVES 1 £15,000
oil
Anthony Eyton RA

133 CHEATER CHEETAH £750
acrylic
Lis Thomas

134 THE DECISION £1,350
oil
Paul Sunderland

135 LIFEJACKET £60,000
gloss paint on paper
Gary Hume RA

136 IRISES £4,000
oil
Jeffery Camp RA

137 LANDSCAPE #1 £680
oil and acrylic on birch ply
Simon Philpott

138 WELL WALK £6,500
oil on oak panel
Sheila Wallis

139 THE YOUNG STEVIE NICKS NFS
hand embroidery
Amy Burt

140 FIRE ALARM £400
acrylic
Nicholas Merrick

141 LIGHTSWITCH (TWO) £250
lightswitch and wallpaper
Jess Wilson
(edition of 75 at £250)

142 NUMBER 256 £360
acrylic
Julian Game

143 COMPETITION FOR NATURAL RESOURCES £2,400
KILLS MORE PEOPLE THAN CIGARETTES
screenprint and acrylic
Violeta Sofia
(edition of 12 at £2,400)

144 VIEW OF ISLINGTON FROM A TENTH FLOOR £9,800
oil
Melissa Scott-Miller

145 A TYGER FOR WILLIAM BLAKE *
oil and acrylic on panel
James Prosek

146 KIM JONG-UN £650
acrylic
Elva Peacock

Refer to sales desk.

147 THREE SQUARE ROOTS ON AN IPHONE £150
digital print on canvas
Ani Setchi

148 CHANCES ARE I MIGHT DISAPPEAR £500
analog photography
Malou Bumbum
(edition of 20 at £250)

149 YELLOWS PAINTING WITH GREEN £2,500
oil and acrylic on linen
Sharon Hall

150 NIGHT CRAWLER £980
oil on linen
Fiona Long

151 ENOUGH £150
digital
Terence Lambert

152 LAST WORK NFS
oil
The late Bernard Dunstan RA

153 HEAD FULL OF DREAMS AND DESIRES £600
oil
Jane Molineaux Boon

154 HOT PANTS (REPLICATION II) £1,800
acrylic and paper on canvas
Juliet James

155 ANDREW GRAHAM DIXON NFS
oil
Cynthia Ward

156 HERSUIT 13/02/2018 14.08 £350
digital print
Clancy Gebler Davies
(edition of 25 at £250)

157 DEPARTURE £6,900
encaustic wax and pigment on board
Terry Setch RA

158 MIDNIGHT MANHATTAN II £6,500
ink and oil on khadi paper
Barbara Macfarlane

159 RIVERLAND: HIGH TIDE UNDER A PINK SKY £460
oil on silver birch plywood
Jackie Fretten

160 LAUGHING WHILE LEAVING NFS
oil on linen
Roxana Halls

161 COLERIDGE £28,000
oil
Sonia Lawson RA

162 GHOST REQUIEM NFS
oil and oil pastel on aluminium
Sean Scully RA

163 TRUMP AND MISS MEXICO £9,000
c-type print
Alison Jackson
(edition of 5 at £9,000)

164 DOES MY BUM LOOK BIG IN THIS? £350
oil
Eleanor Green

165 LA LOGGIA UDINE £16,500
oil
Ken Howard RA

166 FIVE GRAND £5,000
drypoint
Luke Wade
(edition of 5 at £5,000)

167 YOU KNOW WHO £795
oil and acrylic
Lesley O'Mara

168 LOOSE THREADS £4,200
acrylic
Gus Cummins RA

169 BREXIT (MY CAT) £1,500
oil
Polina Semernikova

170 THE ART ISSUE £7,500
sign writers' paint on fridge door
Bob and Roberta Smith RA

171 CARLA £1,995
giclée print
David Shoukry

172 SKELETON MAN £3,600
chromoluxe silver print
Maxime Aliaga
(edition of 15 at £3,400)

173 MOH 8 £480
oil on board
Dan Williams

174 CARNIVAL, PEARLS £4,900
acrylic on photographic print (with Matthew William Habanera wallpaper)
Nicola Green

175 JACOB REES-MOGG £450
oil
Paul Selley

176 REACH OUT (LADDER SERIES) £20,000
oil and wax on canvas
Basil Beattie RA

177 HUNSTANTON NIGHT 1 £350
pigment ink print on Japanese Kozo paper
Yolanda Crisp
(edition of 5 at £260)

178 IT IS WRITTEN £390
acrylic on plywood
Thomas Mcdougall

179 FLAT £850
c-type print
Richard Kolker

180	**WILLIAM JOYCE AND FRIENDS**	£12,000
	acrylic and charcoal	
	Mick O'Dea	

181	**TREE NO. 2**	NFS
	acrylic and charcoal on canvas	
	Tony Bevan RA	

182	**AC16**	£12,000
	oil on linen	
	Sarah Ball	

183	**GARDENER'S WORLD – AUTUMN**	£8,500
	oil	
	Olwyn Bowey RA	

184	**STEPDAD**	NFS
	oil on linen	
	Stuart Pearson Wright	

185	**THE INSPECTION : KIM JONG UN & KIM JONG IL INSPECTING LADY GAGA'S HOMAGE TO DUCHAMP URINAL**	£5,500
	oil	
	David Axtell	

186	**JOYCE HAS ISSUES**	NFS
	oil on gessoed wood block	
	Holland Cunningham	

187	**MY COUNTRY**	NFS
	digital photograph	
	Julie Byrne	

188	**THREE CHAIRS**	£900
	oil	
	Karen Wilson	

189	**MOH 9**	£480
	oil on board	
	Dan Williams	

190	**GRENFELL PYRE AND THE RESCUED FAMILY**	£8,900
	watercolour	
	Shanti Panchal	

| 191 | **LOVE** | £5,000 |

acrylic on ply board
Michael Kirkbride

| 192 | **THE STARLIT SKY** | £1,200 |

oil on panel
Ben Mclaughlin

| 193 | **SELLING ENGLAND BY THE POUND** | £250 |

oil
Peter Ingram

| 194 | **IDENTICAL SHAPES, HALVED AREAS IN REDS** | £20,000 |

acrylic and marble powder on plywood
John Carter RA

| 195 | **THE JOY OF MELANCHOLIA** | £22,000 |

ink
Michael Sandle RA

| 196 | **SANDRA AKA NAN** | £3,000 |

oil
Karl Rudziak

| 197 | **AT THE CHEPSTOW RACES** | £20,400 |

acrylic on board
Anthony Whishaw RA

| 198 | **THE PAIN OF OTHERS (NO. 3)** | * |

ink and acrylic on Dibond panel with aluminium subframe
Idris Khan

| 199 | **FRANZ HALLS EMBODIMENT** | £5,400 |

oil
Anastasia Belous

| 200 | **SEND THEM BACK** | £950 |

c-type print
Sarah Maple
(edition of 5 at £750)

* Refer to sales desk.

201 HER MAJESTY DELIVERS HER 69TH QUEEN'S SPEECH £390

stranded cotton thread on paper

Inge Jacobsen

---

202 GRENFELL NFS

graphite, colour pencil, felt tip pen and screenprint

Maartje Schalkx

---

203 APRIL LANDSCAPE £21,000

oil

Frederick Cuming RA

---

204 HENGE IX £14,000

gouache on paper

Ian McKeever RA

---

205 RICH PEOPLE SMELL FUNNY £1,200

spray paint and oil stick

Jordan Mckenzie

---

206 PLAYING HOUSE £1,000

oil

Guisun Lee

---

207 LAMP BLACK: DIVIDED GROUND £6,900

encaustic wax, raw pigment, ground coal and gesso on canvas

Susan Gunn

---

208 GIMP TO YOUR EGO £1,000

oil

Siomha Harrington

---

209 IDENTICAL SHAPES, TWO ROWS, RED & WHITE £6,500

acrylic and marble powder on plywood

John Carter RA

---

210 ARMCHAIR UNDERDOGS £4,200

acrylic

Gus Cummins RA

---

211 WINTER TERM AT LARA BRISTOL £1,249

oil on panel

Tom Greenwood

---

* Refer to sales desk.

212 STEVE'S B&B (FOUR WINDOWS, THREE DOORS) NFS
acrylic
Julia Abele

213 BIN BAG £6,700
oil on linen
David Agenjo

214 RALPH SMITH: TRAPPER £4,500
oil
Dennis Geden

215 D.F.P. - DECORATED FOR PEACE £350
textile and metal
Eel
(edition of 150 at £225)

216 PORTRAIT OF ROBERT £740
acrylic on canvas board
Myles Dacre

217 PREDELLA (WIDE) £50,000
acrylic
Tess Jaray RA

218 SCHOOL CAT £980
oil on board
Don Cox

219 A PROWLER THROUGH THE DARK £1,500
oil on linen on board
Helen G. Blake

220 BEFORE PARADISE (TRIPTYCH), 2002 £30,000
pigment ink print
Isaac Julien RA

221 VOTE TO LOVE £350m *
spray paint on UKIP placard
Banksy

*Refer to sales desk.

| 222 | **GOOD MORNING MR CORBYN – HOW ARE THE SPEED TRIALS GOING?** | £360 |

digitally drawn archival print
Len Gray
(edition of 40 at £340)

| 223 | **THAT'S WHY I WALK** | NFS |

digital print
Laura Jamieson

| 224 | **FAKE NEWS: THE TRAIL OF TEARS** | £750 |

hand-coloured digital print
Stephen Farthing RA
(edition of 8 at £650)

| 225 | **GIRL IN PINK DRESS** | £4,950 |

oil
Elena Alina Coverca

| 226 | **CONSTANT GROWTH FAILS** | £550 |

oil on panel
Tim Goffe

| 227 | **AFTERNOON AT THE ANGEL** | £1,400 |

egg tempera
Martin Cox

| 228 | **SCREAM** | NFS |

oil
Linda Sofie Jansson

| 229 | **GO GO CHICKS** | £400 |

pen and pencil
Ronald Henry

| 230 | **THE SHABBAT KETTLE** | £1,400 |

oil
Naomi Alexander

| 231 | **VIA CON ME (DREAMING OF YOU)** | £375 |

hand embroidery on vintage photograph
Francesca Colussi

*Refer to sales desk.

232 MATERIAL TENDERNESS £450

free machine and hand-stitched linen cloth, silk, wool and cotton

Michelle Holmes

233 DAY 306, FAKE NEWS: A LOW KEY DAY £750

hand-coloured digital print

Stephen Farthing RA

(edition of 8 at £650)

234 POISED 2 £15,600

acrylic on linen

Paul Huxley RA

235 GRACE £2,200

acrylic on paper

Jane Cattlin

236 PIAZZA SAN MARCO, MISTY MORNING £16,500

oil

Ken Howard RA

237 QUICKLY IN THE AIR £780

oil

Lucia Gomez

238 JOBSWORTH £400

digitally manipulated acrylic print on Perspex

David Hayes

239 FROM SEEDS OF APRIL SOWING £16,000

oil

Philip Sutton RA

240 CASTOR AND POLLUX £12,500

oil

Mick Rooney RA

241 PORTRAIT OF A PARISIAN CAT £980

oil

Stella Parsons

242 EYE OF THE STORM £6,900

encaustic wax on board

Terry Setch RA

243 HWASONG-12 £700
oil
Bernardo Robles Hidalgo

244 PAGE FLICK £360
pencil
Peter White

245 THEN NFS
oil
Lone Huri

246 FALMOUTH, A WINDY DAY £46,000
oil
Philip Sutton RA

247 DOUBLE TAKE (TRAINER) £198,000
acrylic on aluminium
Sir Michael Craig-Martin RA

248 UNTITLED £1,000
household paint, varnish, wax and found materials on board
J. F. K. Turner

249 TWO £500
acrylic on paper
Simon Richardson

250 UNTITLED (LONG ENGINE NO. 2) £36,000
paint and ink on paper
George Widener

251 THE GARDEN OF VENUS £1,200
acrylic and paper on canvas
Juliet James

252 MELTS INTO AIR £21,600
oil
Fiona Rae RA

253 HERSUIT 13/02/2018 17.01 £350
digital print
Clancy Gebler Davies
(edition of 25 at £250)

| 254 | **THE GENTLE TOUCH** | £2,500 |

oil
Nicholas Peall

| 255 | **THE STONES OF VENICE CA' FOSCARI 2** | £45,000 |

acrylic
Joe Tilson RA

| 256 | **EMMA** | £1,500 |

pastel
Nina Danilenko

| 257 | **EMMELINE** | £375 |

hand embroidery on vintage postcard
Francesca Colussi

| 258 | **EUROPE RUNNING THROUGH MY VEINS** | £790 |

embroidery thread, cheese cloth and neoprene board
Tisna Westerhof

| 259 | **COAST 1** | £2,400 |

oil on panel
Kate Sherman

| 260 | **NIGEL FARAGE MEP** | £25,000 |

oil
David Griffiths

| 261 | **THE WELL** | £5,500 |

Flashe, acrylic and oil pastel
Sophie Lourdes Knight

| 262 | **LAMPPOST** | £800 |

acrylic
Matthew Mifsud

| 263 | **CADMIUM LIGHT SWATCHES** | £300 |

oil on linen
Imogen Wetherell

| 264 | **EXHIBITION OPENING: DOUBLE PERSPECTIVE #1** | £750 |

gouache on paper
Anna Shapiro

| 265 | **INFINITY** | £58,500 |

acrylic on canvas, Xirallic colour and fibreglass
Olga Lomaka

266 MAP MUNDI I £6,200
embroidery
Renata Adela

267 DAWN OVER SNOW, LLWYNHIR £8,000
oil
Diana Armfield RA

268 UNTITLED BUILDING £400
pencil
Albert

269 RUNNER £650
oil
Jane Hooper

270 ANTHONY EYTON RA £1,000
oil
David Newens

271 POET £10,000
acrylic
John Wragg RA

272 NONCHALANTLY LEANING £650
acrylic
Jonathan Bennett

273 AQUA ALTA, VENICE £32,500
oil
Ken Howard RA

274 MY FIRST DAY AT THE NEW SCHOOL SEEMED £7,500
TO BE GOING RATHER WELL
ink and crayon
Glen Baxter

275 CURTAIN CALL £6,550
gouache and tempera on paper
Mick Rooney RA

276 PORTRAIT, 1ST DAY ARRIVAL 2015 £10,000
acrylic on board
David Tindle RA

277	**OUTCASTS** *acrylic* Michael Kennedy	£1,850
278	**PENINSULAR** *oil* Jeffery Camp RA	£30,000
279	**BLACK SEA – PEEL SOUND** *mixed media on paper* Barbara Rae RA	£32,000
280	**TULIP DAYS** *oil* Philip Sutton RA	£12,000
281	**PAVILION EREHWON** *gouache* Gus Cummins RA	£4,200
282	**THE STONES OF VENICE CA CONTARINI FASAN** *acrylic* Joe Tilson RA	£45,000
283	**IN THE PARK OF DELIGHTS AND** **DIFFICULTIES (MIDDLE PANEL),** **HELL ON EARTH (RIGHT PANEL),** **HEAVEN ON EARTH (LEFT PANEL) (TRIPTYCH)** *oil on linen* Emma Haworth	£5,500
284	**KEN HOWARD OBE RA** *oil* Tim Hall	£85,000
285	**FLORAL POSING** *oil* Jeffery Camp RA	£4,000
286	**MOVING ON** *acrylic and mixed media on collaged canvas* Frank Bowling RA	£135,600
287	**FASCINATING RHYTHM** *acrylic* Holli Mae Johnson	NFS

288 THE MOANING GEEZER (AFTER LEONARDO) £350
digital print on archival paper
Anna Grayson
(edition of 100 at £120)

289 MOONSTRUCK MAIDENS £4,250
gouache and tempera on paper
Mick Rooney RA

290 IF YOU DON'T KNOW HOW I FEEL, THEN I WILL £5,500
MAKE SURE YOU CAN SEE IT
oil
Evelyn Jean

291 PETER HITCHENER CHANNEL 9 MELBOURNE £18,000
encaustic on board
Bob Parks

292 UNTITLED (WATCH FRAGMENT YELLOW) £48,000
acrylic on aluminium
Sir Michael Craig-Martin RA

293 SUNLIGHT AND SHADOWS £595
freehand machine embroidery
Alison Holt

294 HOPE £1,500
acrylic and resin
Alan Dunne

295 THE TIRED BUSINESSMAN £2,500
oil
Richard Sorrell

296 PITCH I £2,000
oil
Vanessa Jackson RA

297 NUDE AT THE BATHROOM MIRROR NFS
oil
The late Bernard Dunstan RA

298 SECOND GHOST £18,000
acrylic
Mali Morris RA

| 299 | **MAGIC GARMENT** | £21,600 |

oil
Fiona Rae RA

| 300 | **KLIMT IN THE CARE HOME** | £350 |

digital print on archival paper
Anna Grayson
(edition of 100 at £120)

| 301 | **HAPPY DAYS** | £3,600 |

oil on linen
Michael Roberts

| 302 | **DOOR TO THE BATHROOM, LLWYNHIR** | £8,000 |

oil
The late Bernard Dunstan RA

| 303 | **SYRRUS, A FOX AND LUPESTRIPE, A WOLF HAVING A BARBECUE AT HOME IN LEEDS. (FROM THE SERIES, 'AT HOME WITH THE FURRIES')** | £650 |

giclée print
Tom Broadbent
(edition of 5 at £500)

| 304 | **ISHBEL** | NFS |

oil
Chantal Joffe RA

| 305 | **MARINA PISA** | £6,500 |

acrylic on board
David Tindle RA

| 306 | **A GALLERY OF GOLD BOXES: THE GILBERT COLLECTION, SOUTH KENSINGTON** | £7,500 |

acrylic
Stephen Farthing RA

| 307 | **HORSE ON PIANO** | £5,500 |

oil
Anthony Eyton RA

| 308 | **MONDAY WTF?!** | £950 |

oil and acrylic
Steven Ingman

309	**THE QUEEN IN 'GRAYSON PERRY'S' COAT**	£1,010
	acrylic	
	Sudjadi Widjaja	
310	**LEG, SNAILS AND PEACHES NO. 72, POP MAGAZINE, ISSUE 38, SPRING/SUMMER 2018, LONDON 2018**	£15,000
	giclée print	
	Juergen Teller	
	(edition of 5)	
311	**CAUGHT BY FROST**	£7,500
	oil	
	Diana Armfield RA	
312	**ICE FLOES – PEEL SOUND**	£72,000
	mixed media on canvas	
	Barbara Rae RA	
313	**ROUGE**	£4,500
	oil	
	Jeffery Camp RA	
314	**NASTURTIUMS WITH THE LAST OF THE PHLOX**	£8,000
	oil	
	Diana Armfield RA	
315	**BOTTYCELLI DOES GLASTO, TOOTHBRUSH, CONDOM, LIGHTER AND A PACKET OF MINTS**	£3,000
	acrylic	
	Linda Burrows	
316	**THE KEY**	£1,200
	eggshell paint on plywood relief	
	Fabian Peake	
317	**SOLONG SALON**	£32,000
	oil	
	David Remfry RA	
318	**BATTENBERG STUDY NO. 289**	£850
	acrylic	
	Ian Ryan	

319 **LANDSCAPE PORTRAIT** £1,200
acrylic
Amy Gear

*For details of Brian Catling RA's performance piece,
'Fallen Angel', please visit our website at royalacademy.org.uk*

320	**MEMORY**	£14,000
	oil and acrylic	
	Lisa Milroy RA	
321	**UNTITLED (NO. 18) (FROM THE SERIES GREAT FALLS)**	£5,000
	pigment print on Dibond	
	Justin Newhall	
	(edition of 5 at £5,000)	
322	**FOR JOCK SCOT**	NFS
	acrylic on linen	
	Kosmo Vinyl	
323	**DOME OF THE ROCK, FAÇADE**	£120,000
	acrylic	
	Ben Johnson	
324	**WATER**	£144,000
	gloss paint on paper	
	Gary Hume RA	
325	**RONNIE**	£1,250
	35mm digital c-type print	
	William Marsden	
	(edition of 5 at £500)	
326	**BRONZE MANNIKIN**	£18,000
	oil	
	Humphrey Ocean RA	
327	**5 COLOURPAINTING 1**	£2,900
	acrylic on birchfaced plywood	
	Nigel O'Neill	
328	**5 COLOURPAINTING 3**	£2,900
	acrylic on birchfaced plywood	
	Nigel O'Neill	

329 CHROMATOLOGY 2 £18,000
gloss and matt paint on Dibond
David Batchelor

330 BOY LOOKS AT ROCK ON TOP OF ANOTHER ROCK £1,100
archival pigment print on canson
Marion Coutts
(edition of 10 at £950)

331 PARTY £250
c-type print
Miyako Narita
(edition of 25 at £190)

332 HUGO (PORTRAIT OF THE POET HUGO WILLIAMS) £16,000
gouache on paper
Humphrey Ocean RA

333 BEEHIVES IN SNOW, LITTLE SPARTA £28,000
oil paint and wax
Eileen Hogan

334 LIBBY HEART £200
polychrome terracotta relief
Sophy Dury

335 WRESTLING WITH ANGELS *
oil
Mark Alexander

336 SWIFT BLUE £2,500
oil on aluminium
Ben Ravenscroft

337 UNTITLED £2,500
oil and varnish
Tim Balaam

338 RUST ON PEARL £5,000
oil and acrylic
Haider Mannan

Refer to sales desk.

339	**THE WORLD AND HIS WIFE**	£2,950
	oil on linen	
	Suzanne Baker	

340	**MAN OF MERIT**	£2,100
	acrylic, charcoal and lacquer	
	Fiona White	

341	**THE READER'S DIGEST FAMILY ENCYCLOPEDIA OF WORLD HISTORY**	£10,000
	toner on paper mounted on panel	
	Kasper Pincis	

342	**AFTER**	£285
	oil	
	Andy Finlay	

343	**XI FAITH**	£10,450
	oil	
	Ramiro Fernandez Saus	

344	**FOREST**	£3,200
	fabric	
	Unga (Broken Fingaz)	

345	**BURNING MAN**	£2,500
	fabric	
	Unga (Broken Fingaz)	

346	**INTRIGUE**	£16,000
	acrylic	
	Paul Tonkin	

347	**MONOCHROME ISOMETRIC WEAVE**	£750
	paint on ribbon	
	Grace Mcmurray	

348	**OWL BE WATCHING YOU**	£250
	acrylic	
	Mo Noonan	

349	**SARGE**	£1,650
	acrylic on board	
	Magda Archer	

350	**CHARLIE**	NFS
	acrylic	
	C. James	

351	**THE BORED HORSE**	£150
	acrylic	
	Henry Bateman	

352	**THREE WISE MEN**	£400
	oil	
	Ruth Daly	

353	**BLACK SWAN**	£500
	oil on paper	
	Paramita Palchaudhuri	

354	**MAMA WINNIE**	£3,000
	oil	
	Deborah Gilbert	

355	**NOT THE GINGER MAN**	£250
	oil	
	Filomena Sorrentino	

356	**UNTITLED**	£250
	oil paint on board	
	Bob Deakin	

357	**UNTITLED – MOTIF**	£1,000
	oil	
	Ashley Collin	

358	**LIGHT FROM A DEAD STAR**	£4,500
	oil and gesso	
	Lee Wagstaff	

359	**GREEN WHISTLE**	£5,000
	oil on aluminum	
	Ben Ravenscroft	

360	**CALTON HILL**	£1,150
	digital print and hand-painted acrylic	
	Jock McFadyen RA	
	(edition of 40 at £900)	

361 UNTITLED £3,000
oil and spray paint
Tim Balaam

362 TUMBLEWEED AND STONES £6,000
acrylic
Gerard Hemsworth

363 DUSTY £500
watercolour
Una Stubbs

364 REGENERATION £395
oil
Susan Williams

365 THE SHELLEY ROAD NFS
oil
Brian Smith

366 WHITBURN ORANGE MULTI £390
c-type photographic print
James Berrington
(edition of 5 at £350)

367 SELF PORTRAIT IN SCOTLAND £2,500
pencil
Oscar Farmer

368 SUMMER, SCOTLAND £2,000
oil
Sarah Armstrong-Jones

369 SPRING £3,000
oil
Sarah Armstrong-Jones

370 QUEEN SEZ HI! £750
watercolour
Harry Hill

371 DEAD END £350
oil
Nigel Denton

372 UNTITLED £1,200
acrylic and oil pastel
Elizabeth Power

373 SANCERRE VINES £750
oil on board
Martin Hammond

374 PORTRAIT OF JONAH NFS
acrylic
Rosamund Portus

375 THE MEASURE OF A MAN (MY FATHER) £350
charcoal and graphite on wood
Matthew Wilson

376 LAUGHARNE – WHERE A POET IMAGINES £250
acrylic
Marion Thomas

377 TELEVISION OVERBORED £5,000
oil and collage on canvas
Michael Horovitz

378 WINTER GARDEN £975
acrylic
Sarah Constable

379 UNAFRAID – WW2 LOOKOUT, FLOWERS £475
BARROW, DORSET
oil on board
Dick Hewitson

380 NAIL HOUSE 3 £650
oil
Laura Hudson

381 TOWER (BLACK) £775
acrylic on wood panel
Johanna Melvin

382 OLD WOMAN PICKING UP A HAT £550
pen and ink on emulsion-painted MDF
Michael Hayter

383 A LANDSCAPE FOR HIERONYMUS BOSCH
acrylic
John Fitzmaurice
£5,000

384 UNTIL YOU'RE BLUE IN THE FACE
oil
Lucienne O'Mara
£1,000

385 LOCOMOTIVE WHIPPY
colour pencil on card
Elliot Dodd
£1,750

386 BLUE GATES NO. 3
oil on board
Anthony Williams
£350

387 CAPTURING TIME
acrylic on linen
C. Morey de Morand
£3,150

388 A MAZED (LADDER SERIES)
oil and wax on canvas
Basil Beattie RA
£15,000

389 MOVE THE SHADOW
oil
Fabian Peake
£1,500

390 TIPPING POINT (LIGHT BLUE PERMANENT / IVORY BLACK) #2
acrylic on board
Bryan Lavelle
£995

391 HARRODSBURG GAUGUIN
c-type print
Douglas Wallace
(edition of 12 at £2,200)
£2,500

392 HARRODSBURG 'EVERYTHING ON THE DUMMY'
c-type print
Douglas Wallace
(edition of 12 at £2,200)
£2,500

393 BODY
crochet
Iryna Hauska
£2,900

394 UNTITLED NFS
wire, papier-mâché, newspaper, acrylic, ready mix paint and ironing board
Jo Kitchen

395 WELCOME HOME, COME ON IN AND CLOSE THE DOOR £5,000
wood
Harry Hill

396 CHRIS £12.5m
air dry clay and acrylic
Joe Lycett

397 THE GAPER £45,000
carved wood, paint, glass and embroidery
Annie Whiles

398 TOTEM POLE NFS
oil on wood
Vera Christine Heyer

399 RON £800
papier-mâché
Emmely Elgersma

400 THE CONSTANT NEED FOR APPROVAL £9,000
acrylic, LEDs and powder-coated aluminium
James Burke
(edition of 5 at £9,000)

401 BOLLYWOOD GANGSTAS £2,975
felt, beads and mixed media
Helen David

402 ROLLERS £350
archival inkjet print
Mark Denton
(edition of 50 at £200)

403 OFF £310
giclée print
Michael Lowers
(edition of 40 at £240)

404 CAUGHT £310
giclée print
Michael Lowers
(edition of 40 at £240)

405 BLEEDING HEART £20,000
costume jewellery and glass beads mounted on wood backboard
Bruce Hardwick

406 BRAND WARS £1,000
acrylic
Chris Mccrae

407 BUNNY £1,500
oil
Peter Jones

408 BONZO'S DAD £805
silver foil biscuit wrappers
Robert Mach

409 FITTING £1,600
oil
Sofia Mitsola

410 COWCADDEN £3,800
acrylic
Paul Crook

411 VANISHING POINT* 3 £9,600
encaustic, acrylic sheet and paper pattern templates
on plywood
John Atkin

412 THE STONES OF VENICE, CA' CONTARINI FASAN £4,400
inkjet print, screenprint and carborundum
Joe Tilson RA
(edition of 30 at £3,400)

413 THE STONES OF VENICE, CA' FOSCARI 2 £4,400
inkjet print, screenprint and carborundum
Joe Tilson RA
(edition of 30 at £3,400)

414 SOON, NOT YET, TOMORROW £225
screenprint
Martin Grover
(edition of 50 at £150)

415 FREEDOM (VICTORIOUS SECRETS) £2,400
colour pencil
Azita Moradkhani

416 MARK (VICTORIOUS SECRETS) £2,400
colour pencil
Azita Moradkhani

417 THE GOOD SOLDIER £19,000
bronze
William Tucker RA
(edition of 6 at £19,000)

418 VICTORY B £7,800
charcoal on paper
William Tucker RA

419 EGGY POP
£6,000
eggshells reinforced with fibreglass
Gary Miller

420 VICTORY 1
£7,800
charcoal on paper
William Tucker RA

421 GENIE OUT OF A BOTTLE
£17,000
oil
Sara Shamma

422 UNKNOWN
£200
gouache on board
Mohammed Bangura

423 LATEST NEWS – TWIN GIRLS TURN INTO BICHON FRISES
£400
oil pastel
Simon Stephenson

424 FERGUS
£1,500
oil
Peter Jones

425 KATJA MAYER
£575
oil on linen
Celie Byrne

426 UNCLE BERTIE IN THE JUNGLE (IN HIS DREAMS)
£2,500
acrylic
Johnny Bull

427 CABINET MEMBERS
£400
glass, wood, paint, straw and fabric
Sharon Wilson

428 WHO NOSE
£2,450
canvas, plaster, acrylic and wood
Richard Niman

429 PIGMAN
£3,000
marble, granite, prosthetic eyes and chain
Mu Tian
(edition of 5 at £3,000)

430 BEARDMAN £3,000

marble, granite and chain

Mu Tian

(edition of 5 at £3,000)

431 SCIENCE WITHOUT RELIGION IS LAME, RELIGION WITHOUT SCIENCE IS BLIND £15,000

carbon pencil

Beatrice Haines

432 ELSIE FROM SOUTHSEA £650

acrylic

Lizzie Wagstaff

433 BLUE FANDANGO £2,250

oil

Philippa Tunstill

434 INTERIOR NFS

oil on linen

Qingsheng Gao

435 BUBBLEGUM £350

archival inkjet print

Mark Denton

(edition of 50 at £200)

436 RED BEAR £14,500

carpet and mixed media

Debbie Lawson

437 UNDER SIEGE £9,800

collage

David Mach RA

438 FIREWORKS £9,000

watercolour

Jill Mcmanners

439 AND YET MORE ANGRY GREW THE SEA £5,600

paper collage with UVA filter

Ambrosine Allen

440 WE WERE SISTERS IN THE SAME CLASS £12,000

oil

Alan Stewart

441	**SELF-PORTRAIT: THERE'S MORE TO US THAN MEETS THE I...**	NFS
	acrylic	
	Shivraj Singh	

442	**BALLAD OF JAG, TIGER TAMER**	£3,250
	acrylic, charcoal, oil pastel and lacquer	
	Fiona White	

443	**ONCE UPON A TIME**	£22,000
	oil	
	Philip Sutton RA	

444	**ELDERLY DOG**	£900
	oil on board	
	Sally Muir	

445	**BRANDED, LOGO'D & ART'D CAPITAL**	£950
	paper collage	
	Marcus Bowcott	

446	**VENUS**	£495
	oil on board	
	Caroline Yates	

447	**MAINLY PORCELAIN I**	£6,800
	fragmented porcelain	
	Cathy Lewis	

448	**SILVER SWANS BALLET CORPS**	£2,200
	enamel on aluminium	
	Geraldine Swayne	

449	**VILLAGE DOG**	£450
	oil	
	Angeliki Boletsi	

450	**AVIARY: THE WOLSELEY**	£26,000
	sepia ink, gouache and gold leaf	
	Adam Dant	

451	**FIRE**	£600
	acrylic and watercolour on paper	
	Won Young Chang	

452 TWO CHILDREN AND DOG   £1,200
oil on panel
Robert E. Wells

453 BEETLE (BLUE HUB-CAPS)   £4,500
oil on board
Robert Dukes

454 QUIET VENGEANCE   £1,800
oil on gesso panel
Bobbie Russon

455 MEMBERS ONLY   £28,500
collage
David Mach RA

456 DESIRE   £2,000
mixed media
Susanna Blunt

457 THE REAL THING   £2,000
mixed media
Susanna Blunt

458 A LIFES RESTRCTION – RELATIONSHIPS   £1,500
silicone, hair, oil, glass eyes and Perspex frame
Ruth Collett

459 METEORITE   £8,500
oak and nails
David Mach RA

460 MAINLY PORCELAIN II   £6,800
fragmented porcelain
Cathy Lewis

461 WE CAN DO IT   £1,200
ink and collage on board
Jennie Jewitt-Harris

462 HEAD OF R.P.   £1,800
charcoal
Michael Minas

463 WITH A HANDICAP LIKE YOURS...   £25,000
oil
Lucy Jones

464	**PSYCHO DOLLY**	£1,200
	charcoal and collage on paper	
	Jennie Jewitt-Harris	
465	**TRANSFORMING LANDSCAPE PAINTING AFTER JOHN CONSTABLE (150 MINUTES)**	£84,000
	film, monitor with player and frame	
	Rob and Nick Carter	
	(edition of 12 at £84,000)	
466	**DAWN CHORUS**	£15,500
	mixed media	
	Kenneth Draper RA	
467	**PROXIMITY TO YOUR RESPONSE TO HIM, TO THEM, TO HER**	£1,000
	acrylic and spray paint on paper	
	Elizabeth Chisholm	
468	**SIXTEEN**	£300
	acrylic	
	Jenny Clarkson	
469	**FOR THE MANY**	£300
	pen and ink	
	Beth Rodway	
470	**RADIOWAVES AT SEA**	£1,000
	acrylic	
	Jemma Gudgin	
471	**TWELVE MONTHS HARD LABOUR (JANUARY)**	£1,200
	ball point pen	
	Paul Grady	
472	**BOY ON HIS BED**	£12,800
	oil on board	
	Julian Bailey	
473	**DOG**	£1,500
	wood, plaster and paint	
	Mark Croxford	
474	**HALF TIMBER**	£20,000
	oil	
	Humphrey Ocean RA	

475	**GOLDEN GHOST III**	£3,950
	acrylic on paper	
	Mali Morris RA	
476	**TWO OVER FOUR (LEMON)**	£2,500
	acrylic on paper	
	Mali Morris RA	
477	**FLAT LINE (TWENTY SIXTEEN) (GRAVITY) (SECRETS OF THE SAND) (TRIPTYCH)**	£2,900
	woodcut	
	Ade Adesina	
	(edition of 30 at £2,400)	
478	**FLAT BLOCK**	£2,995
	oil on panel	
	Matt Falle	
479	**UNTITLED AK17**	£10,500
	mixed media on paper	
	Rebecca Salter RA	
480	**CROSS ROAD BLUES (HOUSTON)**	£5,500
	c-type print	
	Oli Kellett	
	(edition of 5 at £4,500)	
481	**DIVIDED GROUND: BOMBAY ORANGE**	£16,500
	beeswax natural, raw earth pigment and traditional gesso on canvas	
	Susan Gunn	
482	**LE VILLAGE HOLLANDAIS**	£45,000
	oil	
	Jock McFadyen RA	
483	**NOT FIT FOR PURPOSE**	£26,400
	oil stick on paper	
	Michael Landy RA	
484	**DEJAVU**	£2,900
	acrylic on linen	
	Sooyoung Chung	

485	**YESTERDAY**	£15,000

acrylic on canvas, paper and grooved vinyl
Morgan Howell

486	**ACHILLEA**	NFS

graphite and pencil on Yuki Gampi
Georgia Moors

487	**FENCE (HUMAN)**	£7,750

steel wire
Arthur Analts
(edition of 4 at £7,750)

488	**DRAWING 1753**	£6,900

charcoal and acrylic
Nigel Hall RA

489	**DRAWING 1754**	£6,900

charcoal and acrylic
Nigel Hall RA

490	**CARBON ECLIPSE**	£6,000

carbon fibre
Peter Newell Price

491	**KARMIC SWEETSHOP**	£9,000

light bulbs and sweets on hand-made wooden frame
Daniel Hogg

492	**IT WOULD BE FUNNY IF IT WASN'T TRUE**	£4,500

gloss paint on wood panel
James Joyce

493	**NEW WORLD**	£3,000

painted wood and metal
Nicky Hirst

494	**ROSE100**	£900

screenprint
Philip Byrne
(edition of 5 at £450)

495	**SPIRAL**	£240

etching
Cordelia Cembrowicz
(edition of 25 at £220)

496 CORONA V £2,100

autostereoscopic lens
Lawrie Hutcheon
(edition of 7 at £2,100)

497 MOON MIRROR 42 £850

screenprint on mirror
Amy-Jane Blackhall
(edition of 30 at £850)

498 ELEMENTAL I £375

laser engraving
Amy-Jane Blackhall
(edition of 25 at £300)

499 ENTRANCE TO A MIGHTY CAVERN £1,200

paper collage with UVA filter
Ambrosine Allen

500 GUILT EDGE £600

56 razor blades with applied gold leaf
Maree Hensey

501 SPOTLIGHT ON THE HOMELESS £950

oil
Chris Madeley

502 GNASHER £9,000

wood, metal objects and nails
Timothy Blewitt

503 PIETA1: PLAYING DEAD £18,000

jesmonite, resin, oil, woollen blanket and modelling stand
Cathie Pilkington RA
(edition of 3 at £18,000)

504 FULL METAL JACKET £82,000

oak and nails
David Mach RA

505 VOLUTE V £36,000

bronze
Paul de Monchaux
(edition of 7 at £36,000)

506 W. G. GRACE £14,500
bronze
James Butler RA
(edition of 10 at £14,500)

507 THE QUEEN £132,000
painted fibreglass
John Humphreys
(edition of 3)

508 HER MAJESTY QUEEN ELIZABETH, £17,500
THE QUEEN MOTHER
bronze
James Butler RA
(edition of 10 at £17,500)

509 RUFUS 3RD £12,000
wood, metal and costume jewellery
Timothy Blewitt

VI

518 FORBIDDEN CITY £4,000

3D model:pen and ink drawing printed on layered acrylic
with option of internal illumination
Laurie Chetwood

519 BEWARE OF THE ROCK!
NEWFOUNDLAND VIEW £9,000

acrylic
The late Will Alsop RA

520 I WISH I WAS AT HOME NOT NEAR
NEWFOUNDLAND £9,000

acrylic
The late Will Alsop RA

521 THE ECOLOGICAL LANDSCAPES FOR URBAN £1,000
RESILIENCE

card
Studio 8 Architects

522 ASHTON MARKET HALL NFS

timber and Perspex
Patel Taylor

523 PROPOSALS FOR THE 'UNLOCKING NFS
PENTONVILLE' PROJECT

timber and mixed media
Sarah Wigglesworth Architects

524 A NEW MILTON KEYNES HOMESTEAD STUDY NFS
MODEL

jesmonite
Metropolitan Workshop LLP

525 THE PARLIAMENTARY CAMPUS OF GOD'S £4,000
OWN COUNTRY

pine, plywood, greyboard, 3D print and fabric
Matthew Bloomfield

526 CLARNICO QUAY NFS

plywood, card, metallic foil and acrylic
Carl Turner Architects & Jan Kattein Architects

527 55 GRESHAM STREET GRASSHOPPER NFS

cast metal
Fletcher Priest Architects

528 BERNIE SPAIN GARDENS NFS
plaster
Patel Taylor

529 CONKERS AERIAL WALKWAY NFS
(Cullinan Studio)
cardboard and plastic
Edward Cullinan RA

530 15.0169292 NFS
(Martin Williams and Sarah Griffiths)
mild steel
Williams Griffiths Architects

531 TWELVE HOUSES AT CROUCHES FIELD, NFS
HORSMONDEN, KENT
pearwood
Studio DA

532 SIMULTANEOUS NARRATIVES: BACK OF £1,300
HOUSE SECTION
ink on drafting film, acrylic and print collage
Kirsty Mcmullan

533 ITV HEADQUARTERS (SITE CONTEXT MODEL) NFS
(Hopkins Architects)
timber and 3D print
Sir Michael Hopkins RA

534 SELECTED DUBAI PROJECTS: MODULARITY – NFS
FLEXIBILITY, ADAPTABILITY AND GROWTH
(Hopkins Architects)
acrylic and timber
Sir Michael Hopkins RA

535 LUYONG-POLI £1,200
giclée print
Chong Yan Chuah
(edition of 50 at £490)

536 PHILIP AND PATRICIA FROST MUSEUM OF NFS
SCIENCE FAÇADE STUDY
3D print
Sir Nicholas Grimshaw PPRA

537 VEHBI KOÇ FOUNDATION CONTEMPORARY ART MUSEUM FAÇADE STUDY — NFS

3D print
Sir Nicholas Grimshaw PPRA

---

538 CHEER UP OUR CITIES — £600

photographic print
Eva Jiricna RA

---

539 CHEER UP OUR CITIES — £600

photographic print
Eva Jiricna RA

---

540 OPEN UP PROJECT, ROYAL OPERA HOUSE, LONDON — NFS

c-type print
Stanton Williams

---

541 LONDON'S TEN TALLEST BUILDINGS; BUILT AND APPROVED FEBRUARY 2018 — NFS

giclée print
Hayes Davidson

---

542 ITZAMNA DOORWAY AT HOCHOB — £1,000

ink on paper
Edward Cullinan RA

---

543 UNTITLED — £400

giclée print
Stanton Williams
(edition of 50 at £145)

---

544 EMERGENCY HABITAT FOR SEA-LEVEL THREATENED NATIONS_1 — £350

digital print
C. J. Lim
(edition of 50 at £300)

---

545 DATA FIELD — £900

high-resolution digital print, hand-lacquered, over-painted and collage
Gordon Benson RA
(edition of 7 at £750)

546 RECTANGLE £900
high-resolution digital print, hand-lacquered,
over-painted and collage
Gordon Benson RA
(edition of 7 at £750)

547 ACROBATIC RECTANGLE £900
high-resolution digital print, hand-lacquered,
over-painted and collage
Gordon Benson RA
(edition of 7 at £750)

548 DATA FRAGMENT £900
high-resolution digital print, hand-lacquered,
over-painted and collage
Gordon Benson RA
(edition of 7 at £750)

549 FRACTURED DATA £900
high-resolution digital print, hand-lacquered,
over-painted and collage
Gordon Benson RA
(edition of 7 at £750)

550 ACROBAT + SHADOW £900
high-resolution digital print, hand-lacquered,
over-painted and collage
Gordon Benson RA
(edition of 7 at £750)

551 EMERGENCY HABITAT FOR SEA-LEVEL £350
THREATENED NATIONS_2
digital print
C. J. Lim
(edition of 50 at £300)

552 LUMINOSITY £280
digital print
Yael Reisner
(edition of 10 at £260)

553 JOYTOPIAN DREAMSCAPE £2,000
collage
Birds Portchmouth Russum Architects Ltd

554 THE HUMAN RIGHT'S UNIVERSAL LOGO – £260
YET, STILL UNKNOWN – HERE IS THE SYMBOL
AS SUSPENDED INFLATABLE, IN BARCELONA
digital print
Yael Reisner
(edition of 20 at £240)

555 GADGET CITY £1,600
print from ink and watercolour
Sir Peter Cook RA

556 06.15. JULY 2015 TALFOURD ROAD £750
pencil and watercolour
Trevor Dannatt RA

557 VISITING PROFESSOR IN TRAIN £300
biro
Trevor Dannatt RA

558 2CV 3816 OJ47 £600
pencil
Trevor Dannatt RA

559 INNOVATION STUDIO, ARTS UNIVERSITY NFS
BOURNEMOUTH
(Gavin Robotham and CRAB Studio)
mixed media
Sir Peter Cook RA

560 MACEDONIA ANCIENT SITE. £2,000
RESTORATION AND PRESENTATION 1A
(Dannatt Johnson Architects)
drawing/photograph/text panel 29.4x20.1
Trevor Dannatt RA

561 ENGINEERING BUILDING, LEICESTER – NFS
GLAZING DETAILS
digital print
Arup

562 THE SHARD, LONDON BRIDGE TOWER £220
Renzo Piano's hand sketch, marker, pastel and pencil
on tracing paper
Renzo Piano HON RA

563	**LEAF FORMS 4**	£490
	pencil	
	Paul Koralek RA	
564	**LEAF FORMS 3**	£490
	pencil	
	Paul Koralek RA	
565	**LEAF FORMS 1**	£490
	pencil	
	Paul Koralek RA	
566	**LEAF FORMS 2**	£490
	pencil	
	Paul Koralek RA	
567	**URBAN RETREAT**	£500
	print from ink and watercolour	
	Sir Peter Cook RA	
568	**COUNTRY HOUSE**	£700
	print from ink and watercolour	
	Sir Peter Cook RA	
569	**ROTUNDA**	£2,000
	plaster	
	Stanhope Gate Architecture	
570	**BROADWAY TRIANGLE 2020**	£1,000
	laser cut digital print	
	Jack Sargent	
571	**PHILLIP AND PATRICIA FROST MUSEUM OF SCIENCE STUDIES**	NFS
	framed model	
	Sir Nicholas Grimshaw PPRA	
572	**THAMES LIDO**	NFS
	Perspex	
	Lifschutz Davidson Sandilands	
573	**ARCHIVING THE ANTHROPOCENE: A TIMIC TRACE OF FÅFÄNGAN, STOCKHOLM (SCALE 1:200)**	£250
	digital drawing	
	Katherine Scott	

574 CLARE COUNTY LIBRARY & ART GALLERY, NFS
IRELAND
Perspex, 3D-printed high composite powder and resin
Keith Williams Architects

575 LA FONTAINE A LA FEMME £250
(Follie Gioir)
mixed assemblage
Architectural Advice

576 GARDEN PAVILION (ANGELA BRADY, ROBIN £2,400
MALLALIEU AND ANDREW CARR)
3D print on fused glass
Brady Mallalieu Architects Ltd (Angela Brady,
Robin Mallalieu and Andrew Carr)

577 VICARAGE FIELDS NFS
acrylic and card
Studio Egret West

578 BRICKWORKS COMMUNITY CENTRE LOBBY £2,400
concrete and walnut
Brady Mallalieu Architects Ltd (Angela Brady,
Robin Mallalieu and Andrew Carr)

579 ARCHITECTURAL DRAWING ARCHIVE NFS
(DRAWING MATTER) / CANOPY IN
COLLABORATION WITH ÁLVARO SIZA
wood
Hugh Strange Architects

580 FOUR DOORS, FREEDOM AND UNITY NFS
MONUMENT, BERLIN
MDF
Ian Ritchie RA

581 STORYHOUSE NFS
wood
Bennetts Associates Architects

582 RAM BREWERY REDEVELOPMENT HERITAGE NFS
BUILDINGS SECTIONAL MODEL (1:150)
maple, maple veneer and acrylic
EPR Architects

583 BONDED WAREHOUSE, MANCHESTER NFS

cherry wood, polyjet 3D print, engraved frost acrylic and black gouache

John McAslan + Partners

584 HILL HOUSE PROJECT NFS

pear, sapele, stainless steel, wood stain and beeswax

Carmody Groarke

585 MODEL FOR A CLERKENWELL OFFICE £4,200

plywood, timber veneer and concrete

Piercy & Company

586 DEPTFORD CREEKSIDE STUDY MODEL NFS

stained walnut

Metropolitan Workshop LLP

587 FENCHURCH AVENUE NFS

mixed media

Eric Parry RA

588 ROBIN'S WOOD (PRIVATE HOUSE) NFS

(The late Will Alsop RA and aLL Design)

cast iron, wood, acrylic and steel wire

The late Will Alsop RA

589 AN EXPRESSIONIST TOWER FOR KENSINGTON GORE NFS

poplar

Tom Ferm

590 44 LINCOLN'S INN FIELDS, LONDON SCHOOL OF ECONOMICS, COMPETITION DESIGN NFS

acrylic and wood

Penoyre & Prasad (with Diller, Scofidio + Renfro)

591 DESIGN DISTRICT BUILDINGS (PAIR), GREENWICH NFS

Perspex and painted birch

David Kohn Architects

592 5TH BLOCK JAMSIL HOUSING, SEOUL, KOREA (REVISION E URBAN CONCEPT MODEL) NFS

solid oak and plywood

Florian Beigel Architects

593 5TH BLOCK JAMSIL HOUSING, SEOUL, KOREA   NFS
(INITIAL URBAN CONCEPT MODEL)
solid oak and plywood
Florian Beigel Architects

594 DESERT DWELLER   £350,000
wood and CNC sculpting
Matteo Mauro

595 MILL RACE ENSEMBLE, GUILDFORD   NFS
model and hand-drawn prints
Birds Portchmouth Russum Architects Ltd

596 THE UPSIDE DOWN HOUSE   £18,000
spray paint, MDF, Perspex and 3D-printed ABS
alma-nac

597 COLOUR STUDY FOR WALMER YARD   NFS
(Salter+Collingridge)
water-based paint on card
Fenella Collingridge & Antoni Malinowski

598 BUSHEY CEMETERY   NFS
plaster
Waugh Thistleton Architects

599 RESORT HOTEL, MARRAKESH (1:100)   NFS
terracotta-infused plaster and etched brass
Jestico + Whiles

600 RESORT HOTEL, MARRAKESH (1:1000)   NFS
terracotta-infused plaster and laser cut acrylic
Jestico + Whiles

601 BLOB I MARK II   £8,000
solid brass on silicone mould
Farid Karim

602 EVENTS IN THE CITY   NFS
pespex, foam board and acrylic
Felicity Barbur

603 TEXTILE TECTONICS   £5,000
CNC, 3D print and etched brass
Helen Siu

614 RAWLINGS STREET FAÇADE TYPICAL BAY NFS
plaster and laser-cut brass
Haptic Architects Ltd

615 ASPREY BUILDING INC. CABINET GALLERY – NFS
WORKING PAPER MODEL AT 1:50
card, paper and balsa
Trevor Horne Architects

616 A TEMPORAL TOWN HALL – COUNCIL CHAMBER NFS
MAQUETTE
ceramic, bronze, oak and nylon SLS 3D print
John Cruwys

617 1920'S APARTMENT NFS
cast terracotta, walnut, paper and plaster
Knox Bhavan Architects LLP

618 GREEN SHOOTS AGRICULTURAL TECHNOLOGY NFS
CENTRE, KRONG SAMRAONG, CAMBODIA
wood and acrylic
Squire & Partners

619 DUKE OF YORK RESTAURANT NFS
polylactic acid, plywood and brass
Nex—Architecture

620 GLASS CAVE, THE WORLD'S FIRST ALL GLASS NFS
BIOMIMETIC SINGLE-SURFACE VAULT
STRUCTURE WHOSE FORM IS ITS STRENGTH,
IMMERSING VISITORS IN NATURE WHILST
ADAPTING TO DIFFERENT CLIMATES
beech ply, Perspex and 3D-printed PLA
Tonkin Liu

621 SOUTHMERE VILLAGE LIBRARY COMPETITION NFS
(Will Brown and Lynton Pepper)
laser-cut plywood, card and wire mesh
Architecture 00

622 INNOVATION STUDIO, ARTS UNIVERSITY NFS
BOURNEMOUTH
(CRAB Studio)
wood and plastic
Sir Peter Cook RA

623 SIX BEEHIVES £5,850

hand-painted cardboard laminated onto core of
polyurethane rigid foam
Louisa Hutton RA, Matthias Sauerbruch
(Sauerbruch Hutton)

624 CHATEAU LA COSTE NFS

acrylic and timber
Lord Rogers of Riverside RA

625 MIDLAND GOODS SHED NFS

copper, acrylic and wood
Bennetts Associates Architects

626 MACALLAN DISTILLERY, SPEY, SCOTLAND (1:100) NFS

acrylic
Lord Rogers of Riverside RA

627 FAÇADE MODEL, MANSION BLOCK, £1,500
HAMPSTEAD, LONDON

(Ralph Iberle)
cardboard and paper
Sergison Bates Architects LLP

628 BARRETT'S GROVE NFS

laminated timber, clay brick and acrylic
Groupwork + Amin Taha

629 VAUX NFS

walnut, oak and acrylic
FaulknerBrowns Architects

630 PARK HILL PHASE 2 – FAÇADE STUDY MODEL NFS

wood and paper
Mikhail Riches

631 CENTRE DE CONSERVATION DU LOUVRE NFS
A LIEVIN, FRANCE

timber and acrylic
Lord Rogers of Riverside RA

632 TRIFORIUM GALLERIES ACCESS TOWER, NFS
WESTMINSTER ABBEY

steamed beech and phosphorous bronze
Ptolemy Dean Architects Ltd

633 DEFORMING FIBRES   NFS
digitally fabricated wood and paper
Thomas Bush

634 COMPLETION OF URBAN BLOCK   £5,000
3D print
Ondrej Tichy

635 HYUNDAI PAVILION 2018   NFS
VBX2 nano-coating, SLA 3D print and Corian
Asif Khan Ltd

636 COMPETITION-STAGE MODEL FOR LAMBETH PALACE LIBRARY (1:200)   NFS
card and paper
Wright & Wright Architects

637 PHILLIP AND PATRICIA FROST MUSEUM OF SCIENCE AQUARIUM   NFS
framed model
Sir Nicholas Grimshaw PPRA

638 THE SPACES INBETWEEN (EDDINGTON, NORTH WEST CAMBRIDGE DEVELOPMENT, UNIVERSITY OF CAMBRIDGE)   NFS
plaster
Stanton Williams

639 HUSET PÅ SÖDER (MODEL)   NFS
CNCd timber, 3D print and laser-cut Perspex
Aleksandra Kravchenko

640 THE URBAN STADIUM OF THE FUTURE   NFS
mixed media
Populous (with CRAB Studio)

641 AUCKLAND TOWER, THE AUCKLAND PROJECT   NFS
walnut and brass
Níall McLaughlin Architects

642 130 FENCHURCH STREET   £4,000
resin
Farshid Moussavi RA
(edition of 3 at £4,000)

643 ARCHITECTONIC SEQUENCE: FIELD OF 9 £5,000
3D printed high composite powder and resin
Keith Williams Architects

644 TOWER 3, WORLD TRADE CENTRE, NFS
NEW YORK (1:750)
acrylic and timber
Lord Rogers of Riverside RA

645 STUDY MODEL FOR A HOTEL IN THE NFS
MIDDLE EAST
(Foster + Partners)
timber and acrylic
Spencer de Grey RA

646 CHTHONOPOLIS £24,000
mixed media
Nic Clear (with Hyun Jun Park)

647 100 MILE CITY NFS
plaster
Peter Barber Architects

648 ALTERNATIVE PERSPECTIVES ON THE NFS
ALBERT MEMORIAL
resin, gold leaf and plexiglass
DSDHA

649 GOOGLE MOUNTAIN VIEW NFS
(Heatherwick Studio and BIG)
mixed media
Thomas Heatherwick RA

650 15 CLERKENWELL CLOSE, LONDON NFS
limestone, concrete, Perspex and timber
Groupwork + Amin Taha

651 VATICAN PAVILION CHAPEL (VENICE NFS
ARCHITECTURE BIENNALE 2018 MODEL)
timber and acrylic
Lord Foster of Thames Bank RA

652 RE-IMAGINING STRATFORD NFS
3D-printed powder and ABS, laser-cut etched acrylic
and acrylic rods
Hawkins Brown

653 MERCHANT SQUARE BRIDGE NFS
photopolymer resin, acrylic and mechanical parts
AKT II (with Knight Architects)

654 CAMBRIDGE MOSQUE TIMBER TREE STRUCTURE NFS
timber, Perspex structure and acrylic cover
Marks Barfield Architects

655 BATTERSEA ARTS CENTRE (GRAND HALL 1:25 SECTIONAL MODEL) NFS
timber, foam board, card, printed paper and paint
Haworth Tompkins Architects

656 BATTERSEA ARTS CENTRE (GRAND HALL 1:5 LATTICE CEILING PANEL MOCK-UP) NFS
plywood
Haworth Tompkins Architects

657 STUDENT HOUSING AT DYSON, MALMESBURY NFS
laser-cut lime veneer, acrylic, mirror, stainless steel and 3D-printed SLA
Chris Wilkinson RA

658 ST GILES CIRCUS NFS
acrylic and aluminium
Orms

659 DOIG STUDIO – NORTH COAST TRINIDAD IN CLOUD FOREST. STRUCTURAL FRAME STUDY MODEL AT 1:50 NFS
(Aaron Down)
card, polystyrene, timber and plaster
Trevor Horne Architects

660 TOWER COURT, HACKNEY NFS
timber
Adam Khan Architects and muf architecture/art

661 WARMER YARD NFS
concrete, wood and brass
Crispin Kelly & Salter+Collingridge

662 MESH HOUSE NFS
cherry wood and copper
Alison Brooks Architects

663 HALL OF REALMS, PRADO MUSEUM   NFS
     (MADRID MODEL)
(Foster + Partners)
timber and acrylic
Lord Foster of Thames Bank RA

664 OLD SPITALFIELDS MARKET DETAIL MODEL   NFS
(Foster + Partners)
acrylic and timber
Spencer de Grey RA

665 THEATRE OF THE UNEXPECTED   NFS
card and mixed media
Sarah Wigglesworth Architects

666 THE RED HALL – OXFORD NORTH   NFS
acrylic
Fletcher Priest Architects

667 STUDIO MUSEUM HARLEM, NEW YORK   NFS
(Adjaye Associates)
Foamex and acrylic
Sir David Adjaye RA

668 6–8 BISHOPSGATE   NFS
laser-cut acrylic, mirrored solar film and stainless
steel etchings
Chris Wilkinson RA

669 ROYAL VICTORIA DOCK BRIDGE   NFS
aluminium, wood, and plastic
Lifschutz Davidson Sandilands

670 CITIC TOWER   NFS
acrylic and wood
Kohn Pedersen Fox

671 OAKWOOD TIMBER TOWER 1, LONDON   NFS
wood and acrylic
PLP Architecture

672 TOWER OF BIMBEL   £1,500
paper, wood and paint
Jacob Riman

673 POP.U.LATE - MODULAR DESIGN TO ADDRESS THE HOUSING CRISIS £50,000
3D print
ASTUDIO

674 TOWER OF LIGHT, A BIOMIMETIC SINGLE-SURFACE FLUE STRUCTURE WHOSE FORM IS ITS STRENGTH, HERALDING A NEW GENERATION OF INNER CITY ENERGY CENTRES £9,700
paper and chrome plated tubes
Tonkin Liu

675 CHINA RESOURCES HEADQUARTERS NFS
wood
Kohn Pedersen Fox

676 TOUR 888/SKYPOD NFS
laser-sintered nylon
PLP Architecture

677 AL BAHR TOWERS: AL BAHR INVESTMENT COUNCIL HQ NFS
wood, card, Perspex and foam board
AHR/PCKO

678 WHERE ARE MY GLASSES – UNDER (GREEN) £1,750
hand-blown glass and metal
Ron Arad RA

679 WHERE ARE MY GLASSES – UNDER (RED) £1,750
hand-blown glass and metal
Ron Arad RA

680 WHERE ARE MY GLASSES – SINGLE LENS £1,350
hand-blown glass and metal
Ron Arad RA

681 WHERE ARE MY GLASSES – DOUBLE LENS £1,750
hand-blown glass and metal
Ron Arad RA

682 BEEHIVE £6,350
stackable spruce frames with aluminium sheet top, all hand-painted
Louisa Hutton RA, Matthias Sauerbruch (Sauerbruch Hutton)

683 CROSS ROAD BLUES (LA) £5,500
c-type print
Oli Kellett
(edition of 5 at £4,500)

684 UNTITLED £10,000
mixed media
Bill Woodrow RA

685 UNTITLED £11,500
mixed media
Bill Woodrow RA

686 UNTITLED £10,000
mixed media
Bill Woodrow RA

687 BATHERS #3 (DIPTYCH) £6,000
wood, brass and enamel paint
Steve Johnson

688 BEFORE PARADISE £30,000
pigment ink print
Isaac Julien RA

689 BUNCH £420
oil
Jennifer Roberts

690 THE ENCHANTED GROUND £9,000
colour pencil
Andrew Holmes

691 UNTITLED £500
charcoal
Zoe Carlon

692	**MARKING TIME V**	£3,330
	Japanese woodcut and tulip wood	
	Paul Furneaux	

693	**LAXNESS**	£900
	ceramic	
	Bjork Haraldsdottir	

694	**IT'S FAR BETTER TO FACE THE BULLETS THAN BE KILLED AT HOME BY THE BOMB**	£650
	screenprint	
	Helen Gray	
	(edition of 2 at £400)	

695	**THE BATTLE OF BURLINGTON HOUSE**	£9,800
	collage	
	David Mach RA	

696	**CHANGE IN FORTUNE**	*
	aluminium and copper	
	El Anatsui HON RA	

697	**MONITOR**	£4,900
	bronze	
	Stephen Lewis	

698	**HALF-BUILT TOWER BLOCK (MJ)**	£9,000
	acrylic on plywood	
	Richard Woods	

699	**HALF-BUILT TOWER BLOCK (AL)**	£10,000
	acrylic on plywood	
	Richard Woods	

700	**WEAVING (GREEN)**	£10,000
	oil	
	Lisa Milroy RA	

701	**UNTITLED**	£12,000
	mixed media	
	Bill Woodrow RA	

Refer to sales desk.

702 2 MASKS (POLLUX & CASTOR) £5,000

painted bronze casts of polystyrene packaging
Lorsen Camps
(edition of 5 at £5,000)

703 BEFORE AND AFTER £850

oil
Rosemary Cullum

704 WEAVING (BROWN) £12,000

oil
Lisa Milroy RA

705 HUMBUG BROTHERS £11,000

watercolour and gouache
Sean Cavanaugh

706 RECEIPTS NFS

paper receipts and linen thread
Gail Barker

707 OPEN PERCH *

corten steel
Antony Gormley RA

708 PRISON CULTURE £4,500

prison issue buttermilk soap
Lee Cutter

709 ON £1,000

oil on card
Nicholas Allan

710 BLUE HYDRANGEA £1,500

pencil crayon and watercolour on board
Sigrid Muller

711 BLUE COLUMN £2,100

pigment on paper
David Nash RA
(edition of 20 at £1,716)

*Refer to sales desk.

712	**UNTITLED – BLUE & GREEN**	£8,500
	acrylic	
	Bryan Kneale RA	
713	**SLICK WORK 2**	£600
	archival pigment print	
	Richard Wilson RA	
	(edition of 30 at £500)	
714	**SLICK WORK 1**	£600
	archival pigment print	
	Richard Wilson RA	
	(edition of 30 at £500)	
715	**TRIPTYCH IN BLACK 'THE RUNES'**	£12,000
	acrylic	
	Bryan Kneale RA	
716	**UNTITLED – BLUE & ORANGE**	£8,500
	acrylic on paper	
	Bryan Kneale RA	
717	**SLICK WORK 3**	£600
	archival pigment print	
	Richard Wilson RA	
	(edition of 30 at £500)	
718	**MARITSA**	NFS
	oil	
	The late Gillian Ayres RA	
719	**DIVINING ROD**	£600
	pewter	
	Sorsha Galvin	
720	**CHEQUERED FLAG**	£1,000
	gloss on MDF	
	Alexander Lewis	
721	**ACANTHUS #5**	£4,200
	acrylic and pencil	
	Alison Wilding RA	
722	**ACANTHUS #2**	£4,200
	acrylic and ink	
	Alison Wilding RA	

723 ACANTHUS #1 £4,200
acrylic and ink
Alison Wilding RA

724 BLUE WATER £2,820
hand-worked multiple
Hughie O'Donoghue RA
(edition of 10 at £2,340)

725 X £21,600
patinated brass
Alison Wilding RA

726 BALLS £8,200
newsprint and two pegs
Cecile Johnson Soliz

727 MIRROR £1,090
archival pigment print
Suzanne Moxhay
(edition of 40 at £790)

728 WHERE DID YOU GO Prints from the edition
giclée print available for sale
Phillipa Bloom
(edition of 10 at £200)

729 LOST IN THOUGHTS NFS
wood
Sir Tony Cragg RA

730 LOST IN THOUGHT NFS
wood
Sir Tony Cragg RA

731 TRANSITION £2,000
television, video, cement and polystyrene
Felipe Seixas
(edition of 3 at £2,000)

732 RED HOLED COLUMN £60,000
sequoia
David Nash RA

733 HEXAGONS IN ARPEGGIO – HINGED MOVEABLE FORMS £3,300
brass and copper
Willow Winston
(edition of 3 at £3,300)

734 CURIO £900
plaster
Alison Atkins

735 THE OTHER GROVE £10,000
found building site hoardings
Mike Ballard

736 BRONZE TREE STUMP AFTER JACOB DE GHEYN II £96,000
patinated bronze
Rob and Nick Carter
(edition of 12 at £96,000)

737 THE ROCK AND THE ARCH *
steel, ceramic, jesmonite and polystyrene
Eva Rothschild RA

738 PAPER / WEIGHT £3,300
cast bronze and paper
Tim Burrough

739 LEADS & REGLETS II £7,950
oak
Mark Halliday

740 UNTITLED: FEMALE; 2018 *
cement panels over timber framed plywood lined boxes,
steel top part and steel joint
Phyllida Barlow RA

Refer to sales desk.

VIII

741 BLUE OILY SPOKES AND WORSENED SADDLES £12,000
oil on metal
Neil Jeffries RA

742 'EYES FRONT' (15 MINUTES) £50,000
video on 65-inch screen
Allen Jones RA
(edition of 5 at £50,000)

743 UNDERSIDE OF CARDBOARD BOX £1,100
digital photograph
Mike Perry
(edition of 9 at £800)

744 STRUGGLE £250
digital
Terence Lambert

745 THE WOODS WILL TURN, SAWN #16 £850
archival pigment print
Helen Sear
(edition of 50 at £650)

746 RABBEXIT (AN HOMAGE TO BREXIT) NFS
embroidery on fabric canvas
Yimiao Shih

747 BURST (YELLOW) £26,400
oil on aluminium
Angela de la Cruz

748 FOLLOWING LINES -3 £6,000
pastel, crayon, graphite, polyester film and stainless steel
Ann Christopher RA

749 PROTECTOR CONSTANCE | LEITH HILL NO DRILL £4,100
archival digital print
Ackroyd & Harvey
(edition of 5 at £3,750)

750 VENEER ON BOARD £1,200
letraset, oak veneer, MDF and plastic sucker
John Smith
(edition of 10 at £1,200)

751 KINDLING £400
driftwood, emulsion and string
Jane Burdiak

752 DOC_00000200901.PDF £2,009
hand speed-tufted wool rug
(statistics courtesy of the global terrorism database)
Emily Lazerwitz

753 BIBLIO (PIMM) £3,500
oil paint and India ink on rice paper
Jeff McMillan

754 POINTS OF VIEW £15,000
glass pitcher, book and hooks
Richard Wentworth

755 BOUQUET £400
photograph
Jim Clarke
(edition of 100 at £200)

756 FREEING THE BODY £195,000
assemblage of seven black-and-white silver gelatin prints;
based on the 8-hour performance, Künstlerhaus Bethanien,
Berlin, 1975
Marina Abramović HON RA
(edition of 3)

757 AF HOUSE 3 Prints from the edition
gliclée print available for sale
Kathy Prendergast
(edition of 3 at £4,000)

758 AF HOUSE 4 Prints from the edition
giclée print available for sale
Kathy Prendergast
(edition of 3 at £4,000)

759 THE TAXONOMY OF THE CORNFLAKE £900
cornflakes, acrylic cases, Perspex frame and paper index key
Anne Griffiths

760 DIGITAL BORDERLANDS (CLONE STAMP TOOL) £8,450
double-sided acrylic mirror and your digital
images of the artwork
Edward Jones

761 ELEVATED HA-HA £30,000
razor wire, soldered galvanised cable,
steel pipe and steel brackets
Richard Wentworth

762 FOLLOWING LINES – 5 £6,000
pastel, crayon, graphite, polyester film and stainless steel
Ann Christopher RA

763 GHOST FARM OUT OF DEATH VALLEY £700
laser paper engraving and brushed ink
Brian Catling RA
(edition of 35 at £600)

764 LIFESPANS (23 MINUTES AND 22 SECONDS) £192,000
colour high-definition video on flat panel display
Bill Viola HON RA
(edition of 5)

765 WESTERN UNION £7,000
gloss paint on cardboard
Jeff McMillan

766 ACTION PAINTING £102,000
acrylic
Mark Wallinger

767 UNTITLED (1775) £9,240
oil on board
Vicken Parsons

768 UNTITLED (1776) £9,240
oil on board
Vicken Parsons

769 WEN OUT FOR CIGRETS N NEVER CAME BACK NFS

cast bronze with hand-applied patina

Ed Ruscha HON RA

(edition of 40)

770 HUGH CRANE'S PRAYER BOOK £500

laser paper engraving and ink

Brian Catling RA

(edition of 25 at £400)

771 AN OLD FLAME (CORRECTION) £1,500

mixed media

Anthony Murphy

772 CLIFF CLOTH £2,500

oil and acrylic on paper

Vic Reeves

773 MIS-SPENT YOUTH £5,000

pear wood and steel

Daniel Hogg

774 THE ALL BEING £20,000

paint on driftwood

Richard C. Smith

775 RECLINE, 1PX (STUDY), VERMILLION, 2014-2018 £3,500

2mm stainless steel 202 with hand-painted oil emulsion

Dhruva Mistry RA

776 STUPID WHITE THING NFS

glazed ceramic

Grayson Perry RA

777 UNTITLED (DISPLAY CASE TABLE) NFS

glass and wood

Mona Hatoum

778 UNTITLED (MOTORBIKE) £2,800

fabric, stuffing, vinyl and wool

Terry Williams

779 UNTITLED £13,800

acrylic, plastic, cardboard and glue

Hans-Jorg Georgi

780 LOG-ON £600

wrought iron grate, alder logs, spray paint and emulsion
Jane Burdiak

781 PERGAMON I £5,000

mixed media
David Aston

782 BOOM £3,500

porcelain and black stain
Katharine Morling
(edition of 10 at £3,500)

783 TV WITH DAD NFS

mixed media
Graeme Miller

784 MAENAD £4,250

bronze
Tim Shaw RA
(edition of 12 at £4,250)

785 THE GOLDEN TUTU £5,500

bronze
James Butler RA
(edition of 10 at £5,500)

786 THREE BEARS (MAQUETTE) £9,500

bronze
Laura Ford
(edition of 7 at £9,500)

787 FIGURE ON BALL £3,850

bronze
Tim Shaw RA
(edition of 12 at £3,850)

788 RECLINING MODEL £8,500

bronze
James Butler RA
(edition of 8 at £8,500)

789 STUDY FOR GIFT £7,500

bronze
William Tucker RA
(edition of 6 at £7,500)

790 **LOVELY LION**	£7,400

bronze
Laura Ford
(edition of 7 at £7,400)

791 **THREE CHILDREN ON A BENCH**	£9,500

bronze
James Butler RA
(edition of 10 at £9,500)

792 **HAPPY HORSE**	£365

ceramic
Varla de Milo

793 **SOUL SNATCHER POSSESSION (MAQUETTE VERSION II)**	£17,000

resin, rotting leather and nylon stocking
Tim Shaw RA
(edition of 5 at £17,000)

794 **MARLBORO MAN**	£1,300

wool, waste pipe and plaster
Calum Stevens

795 **DONKEY IN THE DISTANCE**	£45,000

carved wood, paint, glass and hair
Annie Whiles

796 **THE SEVEN STAGES OF DEGRADATION**	£9,750

hand-blown glass and found beach plastic
Sophie Thomas & Louis Thompson

797 **AMARANTHINE**	£1,500

concrete, plaster, metal and plastic
Julie Holt

798 **UNAFFORDABLE HOUSING**	£440

aluminium Dibond and vinyl
Carl Godfrey

799 **THE ALL SEEING**	£18,000

found wood, acacia and mulberry
Richard C. Smith

800 OVERTURNED RIETVELD CHAIR AFTER   *
A SNOW FLURRY

ash and marble resin
Ryan Gander

801 VINCULO DE DOS   £20,000

books and candles
Ana Prada

802 4TH FINGER START (5 MINUTES 37 SECONDS)   NFS

HD video installation (colour, mono sound, continuous play,
synchronous loop) two HD video sources, two HD video projectors,
two speakers
Bruce Nauman HON RA

*Refer to sales desk.

IX

803	**DARK BLOOMS (TRIPTYCH)**	£5,200
	photograph	
	Carolina Mazzolari	
	(edition of 7 at £3,900)	

804	**HENGE VIII (DIPTYCH)**	*
	acrylic and oil on cotton duck	
	Ian McKeever RA	

805	**IN THE MOMENT**	£6,500
	acrylic	
	Mark Habisrittinger	

806	**COLOUR SPACES: COOL WARM WHITE**	£4,800
	acrylic, wood, LED light and colour filter	
	Christina Augustesen	

807	**SPLASH**	£12,000
	acrylic ink on canvas	
	Alf Löhr	

808	**CONSTRUCTIVE INTERFERENCE**	£6,000
	hand-folded polyester film	
	Tony Blackmore	

809	**KINGS COLLEGE HOSPITAL**	£420
	earth	
	Jackie Brown	

810	**JOURNEY**	£360
	3D collaged screenprint and monotype	
	Stella Davis	

811	**HOUSE OF REDLINES**	£300
	pen	
	Dong-Hwan Ko	

*Refer to sales desk.

812 MODULAR ORNAMENT – TILE XI £6,000
ceramic tiles
Joseph Armstrong

813 BOUND (BLACK) £8,000
inlayed spray paint and mirrored acrylic on aluminium
Paul Hosking

814 BOUND (ORANGE/BRONZE) (DIPTYCH) £9,000
inlayed spray paint and mirrored acrylic on aluminium
Paul Hosking

815 CS06 £6,700
steel, fluorescent light and Perspex
Nathaniel Rackowe

816 #1270816 £8,000
charcoal
Jemma Appleby

817 #1130315 £8,000
charcoal
Jemma Appleby

818 UNTITLED (SQUARE CIRCLE) £780
eight colour screenprint with gold leaf
Charles Avery
(edition of 100 at £600)

819 STRANGE NEW WORLD £420
embroidery on giclée print
Rossanne Pellegrino
(edition of 10 at £420)

820 UNTITLED £5,000
ink and spray paint on plywood
Dominic Beattie

821 OUTSIDE THE EDGE £74,000
resin, aluminium and stainless steel
Ann Christopher RA

822 LEARNING TO DRAW £880
ink
Andreas Papanastasiu

823 LIVING £1,400
clock and paint
Junyi Yang
(edition of 2 at £1,400)

824 NO. 755 2017 £22,000
paint on powder-coated aluminium
Rana Begum

825 TO MARS WITH LOVE £6,500
stainless steel
Almuth Tebbenhoff
(edition of 9 at £6,500)

826 LOOKING TOWARDS SCOTLAND, DARIEN £30,000
AND CALEDONIA – FAILURE AND ALIENATION,
BAHIA ESCOCESE, PUERTO ESCOCÉS,
SAN BLAS TRIBAL TERRITORY, PANAMA,
CENTRAL AMERICA
silver gelatin print
Thomas Joshua Cooper
(edition of 4)

827 INCOMING SEAS' EDGE ON THREE £38,000
CONSECUTIVE OCCASIONS AT RANDOM TIME
INTERVALS, SALTBURN JAN 3, 2016,
11:18 - 11:20AM (TRIPTYCH)
graphite and acrylic
Richard Forster

828 SEASONS £1,800
acrylic on paper
James Hurdwell

829 THE GREENHOUSE £430
linocut
Claas Gutsche
(edition of 35 at £390)

830 HARLEQUIN £1,500
gloss paint on aluminium
Alexander Lewis

831 BUTTERFLY
steel and Perspex
Caroline Cary
(edition of 6 at £3,000)

Sculptures from the edition
available for sale

---

832 PARADIGM – B (STRUCTURAL)
weathered steel
Conrad Shawcross RA
(edition of 3 at £66,000)

£66,000

---

833 TEMPORARY FENCE
mirror-polished stainless steel and powder coat
Graham Guy-Robinson
(edition of 3 at £12,000)

£12,000

---

834 HOPE
concrete and line
Aithan Shapira
(edition of 365 at £985)

Prints from the edition
available for sale

---

835 STAR CLUSTER
granite
John Maine RA

£72,000

---

836 OMEGA
patinated bronze
Bryan Kneale RA

£9,500

---

837 FLUTE
patinated bronze
Bryan Kneale RA

£8,000

---

838 UNTITLED (TRISTE)
bronze, plaster, paper and acrylic
Charles Avery

£19,200

---

839 {A VIOLENT INTERSECTION}
reclaimed windows and hand-painted enamel
Michelle Forrest-Beckett

£3,600

---

840 STEDMAN DOUBLES
screenprinted books
Jackie H. Morris

£21,000

841	**PLASTIC FOOTPRINT**	NFS
	recycled plastic and copper wire	
	Jyoti Bharwani	
842	**SQUARE DANCE**	£198,000
	corten steel	
	Nigel Hall RA	
843	**TWIST**	£2,500
	painted steel	
	Sheila Vollmer	
844	**PINK FINISH**	£4,400
	welded steel, thermoplastic coating and gloss paint	
	Jim Unsworth	
845	**FRAGILE**	£3,000
	wood	
	Katie Walker	
846	**EXPANDED NARCISSISTIC ENVELOPE**	£35,000
	aluminium and rope	
	Toby Ziegler	

Lecture Room

847	**FALSE ANGEL ARM**	£7,000
	wood, metal, feathers, Perspex and rubber	
	Brian Catling RA	
848	**SUBMIT TO THE SURFACE**	£7,000
	oil on metal	
	Neil Jeffries RA	
849	**INFANT CHAMBER: JONATHAN RICHMAN, FRANZ SCHUBERT**	£6,000
	oil on metal	
	Neil Jeffries RA	
850	**SLIP LINE: RED, YELLOW, WHITE I**	£3,500
	gouache on paper	
	John Carter RA	
851	**UNTITLED**	£120
	pencil	
	Raymond Anderson	
852	**SLIP LINE (INSCRIBED WITHIN A CIRCLE)**	£16,000
	acrylic on plywood	
	John Carter RA	
853	**INHALE**	£9,500
	oil	
	Vanessa Jackson RA	
854	**SINGER IN THE SQUARE**	£52,500
	oil	
	Bill Jacklin RA	
855	**OUTREACH (LADDER SERIES)**	£15,000
	acrylic, oil and wax on canvas	
	Basil Beattie RA	
856	**SHOOTING STAR**	£70,000
	oil	
	Bill Jacklin RA	

857 REFUGE NFS

copper wire and mixed media

Cathy de Monchaux

858 WINTER SPINNEY WITH BIRDS £27,600

acrylic collage on canvas

Anthony Whishaw RA

859 A WOMAN AND A MAN NFS

oil on wood

Sasha Okun

860 IL LETTO £18,000

oil on linen

Geoff Uglow

861 GEHÄUTETE LANDSCHAFT NFS

emulsion, oil, shellac, lead, metal, clay and gold leaf
on canvas on wood

Anselm Kiefer HON RA

862 NAOMICHI MARUFUJI VS. KAZUCHIKA OKADA £4,200

colour pencil

Tomoyuki Shinki

863 FORTITUDE £12,875

oil

Samantha Parkhouse

864 UNTITLED £200,000

wood and mixed media on canvas

Mimmo Paladino HON RA

865 JULIETTE AND JULIETTE £8,500

oil

David Remfry RA

866 WHIRLPOOL £6,900

encaustic wax on board

Terry Setch RA

867 HOUSE 44 *

pigment and rabbit glue on canvas

Tal R

Refer to sales desk.

868 SHE MOON £80,000
encaustic wax and beach detritus on canvas
Terry Setch RA

869 OPEN HEART *
acrylic
Tracey Emin RA

870 THE STONES OF VENICE CA' FOSCARI 1 £45,000
acrylic
Joe Tilson RA

871 IGNITE £9,500
oil
Vanessa Jackson RA

872 MAN AND WOMAN: ADAM AND EVE SERIES £12,000
acrylic
David Tindle RA

873 WAITING FOR THE SONG £12,000
acrylic
John Wragg RA

874 TIGER TIGER £30,000
oil
Eileen Cooper RA

875 ANGIE AND HER FRIENDS £12,000
acrylic on board
David Tindle RA

876 NIGHT FOLLOWS DAY £2,520
oil on board
Timothy Hyman RA

877 BONNARD DIARY £6,000
oil
Leonard McComb RA

878 THE LAST CIGARETTE £10,000
acrylic
John Wragg RA

Refer to sales desk.

879 INSIDE IT OPENS UP AS WELL NFS

photographic drawing printed on seven sheets of
paper mounted on seven sheets of Dibond
David Hockney RA

880 SEVEN TROLLIES, SIX AND A HALF STOOLS, NFS
SIX PORTRAITS, ELEVEN PAINTINGS,
AND TWO CURTAINS

photographic drawing printed on seven sheets of paper
mounted on seven sheets of Dibond
David Hockney RA

881 SQUALL £42,000

mixed media and pheasant feathers in antique cabinet
Kate MccGwire

882 PISSENLIT 3 £2,400

straw, wire, plaster and fabric
Amanda Benson

883 STEPPING OUT £150,000

fibreglass, tinted acrylic and mixed media
Allen Jones RA

884 PLAYING GOD I £60,000

cast iron
Peter Randall-Page RA

885 PLAYING GOD II £60,000

cast iron
Peter Randall-Page RA

886 SWORD OF ST GEORGE £25,000

Egyptian porphyry and alabaster and English basalt
Stephen Cox RA

887 FIGURE-DEPOSITION £30,000

Egyptian porphyry
Stephen Cox RA

Sackler Galleries

Stairs

888 GREEN VINE £16,000
burnt newspaper, masking tape and cardboard
Tim Shaw RA

889 LE PETIT HENRI – NOT QUITE SO SURPRISED! £800
– AN HOMAGE TO ROUSSEAU
papier-mâché on a chicken wire frame
Peter Flory

North

890 LOTTO, GUNS, AMMO £900
intaglio
Emma Stibbon RA
(edition of 35 at £700)

891 FOREST FIRE £1,050
intaglio
Emma Stibbon RA
(edition of 35 at £800)

892 DEAD HORSE POINT £1,200
intaglio
Emma Stibbon RA
(edition of 35 at £900)

893 DIMINISH 2 £750
etching
Jo Gorner
(edition of 30 at £600)

894 SET £850

intaglio and woodcut
Emma Stibbon RA
(edition of 35 at £650)

895 CANYON DE CHELLY £800

intaglio
Emma Stibbon RA
(edition of 35 at £600)

896 DISAPPEARING INTO 'AS BRIGHTNESS FALLS £500
FROM THE AIR', HEDGE DRAWING 01-18

conté on Mylar
Laurie Steen

897 JINJA ROAD STUDY I £460

hand-coloured etching
Bronwen Sleigh
(edition of 25 at £400)

898 HAAR £14,000

acrylic on board
Anne Magill

899 HAVING A SIT ON A 3D RENDER, THINKING £1,900
OF FISH

pencil and acrylic
Greg Eason

900 NORWEGIAN COD £1,700

pencil
Greg Eason

901 SOLITARY VIEW £250

photopolymer etching
Ross Bullock
(edition of 200 at £200)

902 BETHNAL GREEN LIBRARY £1,000

digital print
Jock McFadyen RA
(edition of 40 at £750)

903 TREELINE £340
etching
Gregory Moore
(edition of 15 at £300)

904 BLACK ROCK – LEVADA DOS BALCÕES £1,400
charcoal
Dominic Zwemmer

905 YOU HAVE TO BE NICE TO PEDESTRIANS, £900
ODESSA #1
archival inkjet print
Richard Davies
(edition of 25 at £800)

906 SNOWBOY £630
etching
Ian Ritchie RA
(edition of 20 at £480)

907 THREE WISE MEN £630
etching
Ian Ritchie RA
(edition of 55 at £480)

908 SELFIE WITH POLITICAL CAUSES £51,600
woodcut
Grayson Perry RA
(edition of 12 at £51,600)

909 ROYAL ACADEMY OF MUSIC OCULUS £630
etching
Ian Ritchie RA
(edition of 30 at £480)

910 SNOWOMAN & SNOWBOY £630
etching
Ian Ritchie RA
(edition of 20 at £480)

911 SKIERS 2 £650
photography
Jon Cardwell
(edition of 15 at £550)

912 BAGNOLI II £875

etching and aquatint
Ros Ford
(edition of 15 at £575)

913 LONBAIN ROCK £750

lithograph and digital print
Zarina Stewart-Clark

914 STELLAR £340

screenprint
Anna Harley
(edition of 40 at £180)

915 AT THIRSK HALL £700

etching
Norman Ackroyd RA
(edition of 90 at £540)

916 BEN MORE £120

etching
Michael Bowman
(edition of 50 at £100)

917 07:13 FROM EUSTON £200

photo etching
Lisa Chappell
(edition of 20 at £150)

918 TO DESIRE WITHOUT AN OBJECT II £2,100

aburidashi-fire etching, acid and water
Kaori Homma
(edition of 3 at £1,995)

919 HAMBLETON IN WINTER £1,300

etching
Norman Ackroyd RA
(edition of 90 at £960)

920 BARRA HEAD FROM MINGULAY £700

etching
Norman Ackroyd RA
(edition of 90 at £540)

921 AT ORANMORE CASTLE, CO. GALWAY £700
etching
Norman Ackroyd RA
(edition of 90 at £540)

922 OMEROS – THE SEA IS HISTORY £12,000
(HOMAGE TO DEREK WALCOTT), 2002/2018
pigment ink print
Isaac Julien RA
10% of payment to the artist goes to the Diaspora Pavilion
and the Khadija Saye fund
(edition of 10)

923 OFF HERMA NESS – SHETLAND £700
etching
Norman Ackroyd RA
(edition of 90 at £540)

924 ON SOAY SOUND, ST KILDA £700
etching
Norman Ackroyd RA
(edition of 90 at £540)

925 SEARCHING FOR A LOST BUTTON AT JACKSON'S £1,545
lithography and screenprint
Chris Orr RA
(edition of 50 at £1,200)

926 THE FAUVES PICNIC £1,175
screenprint
Chris Orr RA
(edition of 50 at £900)

927 DEAD STUFF £295
drypoint
Janet Milner
(edition of 15 at £195)

928 HOW TO EARN AN HONEST CRUST £1,320
engraving
Chris Orr RA
(edition of 20 at £1,020)

929 HOME IS THE SOLDIER, HOME FOR HIS TEA £5,500
watercolour and pencil
Chris Orr RA

930 THE BITS JOHN CONSTABLE LEFT OUT £1,545
lithography
Chris Orr RA
(edition of 50 at £1,200)

931 HOME £400
etching and aquatint
Gavin Iain Campbell
(edition of 50 at £300)

932 ME £250
etching
Thomas Adam
(edition of 50 at £210)

933 YELLOW JERSEY £125
linocut
Cecilia Rouncefield
(edition of 20 at £75)

934 WINTER WALK £425
etching
David L. Carpanini
(edition of 25 at £300)

935 BELLBOY £150
screenprint on mirror metallic card
Jon Butterworth
(edition of 25 at £150)

936 THE SECRET £350
drypoint and watercolour
Richard Spare
(edition of 100 at £275)

937 HALF OF ME WILL ALWAYS BE YOU £5,000
intaglio, paper cut and chine-collé
Marilene Oliver
(edition of 3 at £5,000)

938 PLATONIC SOLIDS £850

etching and hand-marbled paper
Louisa Boyd

939 LINNE £780

Japanese woodblock
Rebecca Salter RA
(edition of 16 at £635)

940 TABULA SERIES 3 £780

Japanese woodblock
Rebecca Salter RA
(edition of 16 at £635)

941 KENZO'S WELL £4,750

watercolour
Ian McKenzie Smith

942 RADICAL GEOMETRY IN THE AGE OF THE POST MODERN £800

brass
Peter Hinchliffe
(edition of 10 at £700)

943 SPATIAL HYBRID 2 £350

screenprint
Brigitte Parusel
(edition of 50 at £220)

944 ENVELOPE £1,300

paper cut
Louise Ockenden

945 ENVELOPE £1,600

paper cut
Louise Ockenden

946 SPORE £300

hand-cut paper
Clare Pentlow

947 URBAN ARCHAEOLOGY £1,750

relief print embossing on hand-made paper
Peter Ford

948 TIME AND TIDE £6,000
screenprint
Sir Richard Long RA
(edition of 25 at £5,100)

949 PALM £300
hand-painted lithograph
Amy Wiggin
(edition of 10 at £200)

950 TRACES £350
photographic print
Liana Allos

951 PALE SHOWERS BLUE £450
etching
Calum McClure
(edition of 10 at £400)

952 WISH ME WELL £575
etching and chine-collé
Lorena Herrero
(edition of 5 at £500)

953 A VIEW OF MATERA £335
etching
Paul Hawdon
(edition of 40 at £285)

954 FIRST MEMORY; KITCHEN 2 £300
graphite
Donna Leighton

955 COMPOSITION III £650
water-based monotype
Tamsin Relly

956 FIRST MEMORY; KITCHEN £300
graphite
Donna Leighton

957 INFERNO Prints from the edition
screenprint and 23 carat red gold leaf available for sale
Tobias Till
(edition of 50 at £3,000)

958 INFLOW £510

paper
Kate Hipkiss

959 CLOCKWORK FOUNTAIN £690

etching and block-print
Katherine Jones
(edition of 30 at £580)

960 THE SCULPTOR 16 £1,400

monotype
William Tucker RA

961 MY BOX! £250

linocut
Jennifer Gill
(edition of 10 at £200)

962 WHITE FIELD AND HAILSTORM 2 £1,800

*writing ink, hailstones (collected during hailstorm
in Bishops Hull, Somerset) and acrylic ink on board*
Deborah Westmancoat

963 THOUGHTLESS CHAMBER: FOUR CHEESE £570

archival inkjet print
Neil Jeffries RA
(edition of 30 at £450)

964 THOUGHTLESS CHAMBER: THRUSH £550

archival inkjet print
Neil Jeffries RA
(edition of 30 at £430)

965 THE MOUNTAIN PEOPLE £160

archival digital print
Tim Ellis
(edition of 50 at £140)

966 ST MARY'S CHURCH, SHOREHAM-BY-SEA £180

linocut and collage
Jackie Gordon
(edition of 11 at £180)

967 GRATER NFS

pen and ink
Kevin Hinton

968 STEVE & VIC (DIPTYCH 01)
giclée print
Philippa Lawrence
(edition of 15 at £800)

Prints from the edition
available for sale

969 TALES FROM THE RIVERBANK 1
cyanotype
Martyn Grimmer
(edition of 30 at £285)

£415

970 UNPARALLELED
screenprint
Basil Beattie RA
(edition of 35 at £900)

£1,150

971 TRASH
three colour screenprint on Amercian dollar bill
Dave Buonaguidi
(edition of 125 at £90)

£125

972 STRIPES AND FACES
pen and pencil on found paper
Dene Leigh

£1,250

973 BRITISH MUSEUM
graphite
Maartje Schalkx

NFS

974 THIS TOO SHALL PASS
paper, fungus and insects
Julian Camilo

NFS

975 ALL AT SEA
digital pigment print
Carol McDaid
(edition of 50 at £150)

£200

976 COLLAGE FOR THE LONG FINGER 4
collaged oil paint on paper
Clare Woods

£2,800

977 ART IS YOUR HUMAN RIGHT
screenprint
Bob and Roberta Smith RA
(edition of 50 at £500)

£575

978 BLUE MOUNTAIN NFS
acrylic on Polaroid
Nicky Hodge

979 STIRP SERIES: WEINHEIMER SISTERS £750
photogenic drawing
Bethe Bronson

980 COLOUR SPLAT EDGE (BLACK) £3,600
screenprint
Ian Davenport
(edition of 25 at £3,200)

981 THE TOPOGRAPHY OF Prints from the edition
CLOTH (DIPTYCH 02) available for sale
giclée print
Philippa Lawrence
(edition of 15 at £800)

982 ROSE WINGS £1,200
inkjet, laser-cut balsa and Japanese tissue
Stephen Hoskins
(edition of 3 at £1,000)

983 OHNE STRAHLEN V (WITHOUT LIGHT) £800
photo etching
Johanna Love
(edition of 10 at £630)

984 I CAN'T REMEMBER BUT I KNOW (DIPTYCH) £3,000
giclée print
Mariele Neudecker
(edition of 24 at £2,700)

985 WHAT UNITES HUMAN BEINGS £575
screenprint
Bob and Roberta Smith RA
(edition of 50 at £500)

986 REDDY BREK £165
giclée print
David Bray
(edition of 10 at £110)

987 AN ENEMY OF THE PEOPLE £250

etching
Kitty Reford
(edition of 10 at £200)

988 ISLAND GARDENS £300

etching
Kitty Reford
(edition of 10 at £250)

989 BLACK DOG PONDERS £150

monotype
Helen Parker

990 OUGHTERARD CILLÍN SAMPLE I £2,600

ink on vellum
Miriam de Búrca

991 UNTITLED (I) £150

gouache on paper
Hannah Eccles

992 WHERE THE WATER MEETS £650

photo etching on hand-made book covers
Victoria Ahrens
(edition of 10 at £550)

993 ASH SHADOW £700

ink on French cotton paper
Lucy Auge

994 SAMPLER £500

screenprint
Toni Davey
(edition of 30 at £430)

995 ORBITERS 6 £2,800

pencil
Jane Harris

**996 FRENCH FANCIES, A YOUNG
TOBY'S DILEMMA** £900

giclée print
Tom Barker
(edition of 25 at £700)

997 FOUR POPPIES £1,300
screenprint
Dame Elizabeth Blackadder RA
(edition of 80 at £1,140)

998 LANGOUSTINE £1,140
etching
Dame Elizabeth Blackadder RA
(edition of 50 at £1,020)

999 TAKING SIDES £22,000
ink
Michael Sandle RA

1000 12 HOURS IN AND WITH THE ATLANTIC £2,300
OCEAN (ENGLAND)
pen, rust, earth and water from the Atlantic Ocean on paper
Peter Matthews

1001 SOPHIE £900
mixed media on digital print
Esmé Clutterbuck

1002 CAPITAL FOLLY (AFTER PIRANESI) £7,200
archival c–type print
Emily Allchurch
(edition of 15 at £6,250)

1003 UNTITLED (WORK FOR KIDS £5,000
FOR KIDS CHARITY)
watercolour
Michael Sandle RA

1004 A HUMUMENT P.257: SCIENCE TELLS YOU TO £475
GO ON
digital print and screenprint
Tom Phillips RA
(edition of 75 at £375)

1005 A HUMUMENT P.146: £475
FROM THE HARD BENCHES
digital print and screenprint
Tom Phillips RA
(edition of 75 at £375)

1006 A HUMUMENT P.325: ONLY CONNECT £475
digital print and screenprint
Tom Phillips RA
(edition of 75 at £375)

1007 A HUMUMENT P.238: DARK WORK AT SMYRNA £475
digital print and screenprint
Tom Phillips RA
(edition of 75 at £375)

1008 ASH TO ASH (STUDY) £575
archival digital print
Ackroyd & Harvey
(edition of 50 at £380)

1009 MIES VAN DER ROHE (DIPTYCH) £5,700
screenprint
Sir Michael Craig-Martin RA
(edition of 30 at £4,200)

1010 GERRIT RIETVELD (DIPTYCH) £5,700
screenprint
Sir Michael Craig-Martin RA
(edition of 30 at £4,200)

1011 EVERGREEN £4,250
oil based woodcut
Katsutoshi Yuasa
(edition of 5 at £3,250)

1012 IMMINENCE £975
Japanese woodcut
Sara Lee
(edition of 25 at £695)

1013 THE PALACE OF THE FAVOURITE, MARRAKECH £625
archival inkjet print
Jennifer Dickson RA
(edition of 10 at £475)

1014 COURTYARD OF THE KARAOUIYINE MOSQUE, FÉS £625
archival inkjet print
Jennifer Dickson RA
(edition of 10 at £475)

1015 FOUNTAIN NEAR THE MAUSOLEUM OF £625
MOHAMMED V, RABAT
archival inkjet print
Jennifer Dickson RA
(edition of 10 at £475)

1016 CASANOVA SELLING THE NATIONAL LOTTERY £990
TO CATHERINE THE GREAT
etching and chine-collé
Stephen Chambers RA
(edition of 25 at £840)

1017 SOMEWHERE £3,750
screenprint
Stephen Chambers RA
(edition of 6 at £3,200)

1018 DOMM £990
etching
Stephen Chambers RA
(edition of 25 at £840)

1019 STUDENT LIFE: MS BEHAVIN' £850
etching with tea stained Gambi chine-collé
Stephen Chambers RA
(edition of 30 at £720)

1020 STUDENT LIFE: MR MEANOUR £850
etching with tea stained Gambi chine-collé
Stephen Chambers RA
(edition of 30 at £720)

1021 A ROOM OF ONE'S OWN – SEASONS £1,360
water-based woodcut
Nana Shiomi
(edition of 30 at £960)

1022 PROGRESSION 4 £1,500
etching
Barton Hargreaves
(edition of 25 at £950)

1023 THE ELECTRIC FIRE £350
linocut
Steven Hubbard
(edition of 50 at £295)

1024 A ROOM OF ONE'S OWN – STILL LIFE £1,360
water-based woodcut
Nana Shiomi
(edition of 30 at £960)

1025 STARS AND SEA AT NIGHT W £15,000
monotype
Bill Jacklin RA

1026 SPATIAL HYBRID 1 £350
screenprint
Brigitte Parusel
(edition of 50 at £220)

1027 APPROACH £750
Japanese woodcut
Sara Lee
(edition of 25 at £495)

1028 HOME? £2,500
pigment print hand-finished in oil and screenprint on paper
Ewa Gargulinska
(edition of 20 at £1,850)

1029 THE EXCHANGE NFS
woodcut
Stuart Coy

1030 THE ALLOTMENT £250
screenprint
Martha Ellis
(edition of 100 at £200)

1031 DIVA £4,100
linocut
Eileen Cooper RA
(edition of 20 at £3,250)

1032 21-XXI NFS
collagraph
Fumiko Nakajima

1033 WHEN THE SEA WAKES INSIDE YOU
lithograph and indigo pigment on Japanese paper and hand-dyed linen
Danielle Creenaune
(edition of 2 at £600)

Prints from the edition available for sale

1034 MY NAME IS NOT COLIN
mixed media and cocktail sticks
Eve Parnell
(edition of 25 at £900)

Sculpture from the edition available for sale

South

1035 MARY DAY
linocut
James Dodds
(edition of 150 at £470)

£570

1036 SWEET CONCILIATION
digital collage
Ana Alalba
(edition of 25 at £270)

£500

1037 PLANE 5
screenprint, gold leaf and copper leaf
Frea Buckler
(edition of 20 at £280)

£380

1038 DARK IN THE PARK
linocut
Rachel Busch
(edition of 12 at £350)

£425

1039 DUTCH BARN
monoprint
Ursula Leach

£880

1040 BENT GLYPH – HOMAGE TO COROT £1,400
linocut on Japanese Kozo paper
G.W. Bot
(edition of 25 at £1,100)

1041 SWISS COTTAGE LIBRARY £370
giclée print
Charles Chambers
(edition of 5 at £280)

1042 LIGHT COMPOSITION 5 £2,000
bespoke sticker on found photograph
Julie Cockburn

1043 THE WILDERNESS CATALOGUE £2,600
oil on panel
Ben McLaughlin

1044 FUNKY PIGEON £300
photograph
Debbie Price

1045 HEAD £350
oil-based ink screenprint
Daniel Augustine
(edition of 50 at £250)

1046 LIGHT COMPOSITION 7 £2,000
bespoke sticker on found photograph
Julie Cockburn

1047 BLUE MOTHER £125
drypoint etching on vintage piano sheet music
Sara Jayne Harris
(edition of 25 at £90)

1048 CLOUD BASE £840
etching
Sandi Anderson
(edition of 20 at £720)

1049 LEARNING TO ACCEPT £720
ink
Andreas Papanastasiu

1050 CONTINENTAL DRIFT –   £325
UNKNOWN HORIZONS
linocut
Adrian Bannister
(edition of 50 at £175)

1051 GRASSLAND GLYPH - PORTRAIT   £1,400
linocut on Japanese Kozo paper
G. W. Bot
(edition of 25 at £1,100)

1052 TOOLS IN A PUZZLED VESSEL   £120,000
(ONE – EIGHT)
eight woodcuts, etchings, lithographs and
mechanical abrasions
Jim Dine HON RA
(edition of 6 at £100,000)

1053 SOMEWHERE IN THE HEBRIDES   £1,000
digital print
Jock McFadyen RA
(edition of 40 at £750)

1054 ELEVEN   £1,000
lithograph
Tess Jaray RA
(edition of 20 at £900)

1055 SUMMER GROWTH   £750
lithograph
Charlotte Verity
(edition of 20 at £600)

1056 SWIMSUIT   £4,500
linocut on Japanese Kozo paper
Marie Harnett
(edition of 15 at £3,700)

1057 BETWEEN THE LINES   £2,500
charcoal and pencil on paper held together with a clamp
Diego Mallo Ferrer

1058 NEW LEAVES £750
lithograph
Charlotte Verity
(edition of 20 at £600)

1059 SNOW FALL £900
screenprint
Samantha Cary
(edition of 25 at £600)

1060 FOX TALBOT'S ARTICLES OF GLASS £3,000
(TAGGED DECANTER)
polymer photogravure etching
Cornelia Parker RA
(edition of 25 at £2,600)

1061 FOX TALBOT'S ARTICLES OF GLASS £3,000
(THREE DECANTERS)
polymer photogravure etching
Cornelia Parker RA
(edition of 25 at £2,600)

1062 FOX TALBOT'S ARTICLES OF GLASS £3,000
(FOUR GLASSES)
polymer photogravure etching
Cornelia Parker RA
(edition of 25 at £2,600)

1063 ACROBATS £380
Japanese woodblock
Julia Peintner
(edition of 35 at £280)

1064 EROS AND THANATOS £620
monoprint
Jean Skeggs

1065 HERE AND THERE OVERLAP £2,400
linocut
Andrew Carter
(edition of 10 at £1,600)

1066 A QUESTION OF EARTH £800
etching
Freya Payne
(edition of 15 at £675)

1067 THE LONELY MAN £800
etching
Freya Payne
(edition of 15 at £675)

1068 HAYWARD III £675
linocut
Paul Catherall
(edition of 50 at £515)

1069 FOX TALBOT'S ARTICLES OF GLASS £3,000
(ALL TOGETHER NOW)
polymer photogravure etching
Cornelia Parker RA
(edition of 25 at £2,600)

1070 STILL LIFE WITH NAUTILUS CUP £5,700
(AFTER FRANS SANT-ACKER, 1648-1688)
archival inkjet print
Gordon Cheung
(edition of 20 at £4,200)

1071 FOCUS MOVING NFS
photographic drawing printed on two sheets of
paper mounted on two sheets of Dibond
David Hockney RA

1072 SEA ICE – NORTHWEST PASSAGE £2,250
carborundum and chine-collé
Barbara Rae RA
(edition of 30 at £1,950)

1073 IN THE FOLD OF THE SEA £550
Japanese woodcut
Carol Wilhide Justin
(edition of 20 at £430)

1074 KINGDOM, COME – ARISE £350
inkjet
Edd Pearman
(edition of 35 at £300)

1075 STEINN £1,200
wax crayon, charcoal and acrylic
Sarah Duncan

1076 COVE £250
giclée print
Paul Martin
(edition of 75 at £175)

1077 AN ACTIVIST ARTEFACT £400
digital collage
Anthony Chun Ming Ko
(edition of 20 at £300)

1078 ICEBERG – BAFFIN BAY £1,450
carborundum print
Barbara Rae RA
(edition of 40 at £1,250)

1079 SEA ICE – DISKO BAY £1,450
carborundum print
Barbara Rae RA
(edition of 40 at £1,250)

1080 SURPRISING ANGLES £900
intaglio
Her Majesty Queen Sonja of Norway
Payments to the artist support the Queen Sonja Print Award
(edition of 45 at £700)

1081 TIMESCAPE £320
etching
Lucy Armah
(edition of 190 at £200)

1082 VENTANA £450
woodcut and archival digital print
Prudence Ainslie
(edition of 25 at £325)

1083	**RAIL SHED, LEIPZIG**	£1,200
	intaglio	
	Emma Stibbon RA	
	(edition of 35 at £900)	

1084	**GLIMPSES OF CATALUNYA**	£330
	photo polymer gravure etching	
	Andy Lovell	
	(edition of 65 at £200)	

1085	**CAULTON'S COTTAGE**	£1,100
	toned silver gelatin print	
	Paul Hart	
	(edition of 12 at £900)	

1086	**HOME**	£890
	graphite and white conté	
	Anselmo Swan	

1087	**PEACH STONES**	£1,350
	linocut	
	Peter Randall-Page RA	
	(edition of 30 at £1,150)	

1088	**BEFORE MY HELPLESS SIGHT**	£470
	relief engraving	
	Neil Bousfield	
	(edition of 50 at £380)	

1089	**WITH WHOM THEIR LOVE IS DONE**	£470
	relief engraving	
	Neil Bousfield	
	(edition of 50 at £380)	

1090	**SELF PORTRAIT AS A BOOK, CYAN**	£450
	screenprint	
	Fiona Banner RA	
	(edition of 50 at £350)	

1091	**MOCK TUDOR**	£875
	pen and crayon on tracing paper	
	Mark Beesley	

1092 THRILLS £500

c-type print
Richard Heeps
(edition of 25 at £395)

1093 UNTITLED (NO. 45) £5,000
(FROM THE SERIES GREAT FALLS)

pigment print on Dibond
Justin Newhall
(edition of 5 at £5,000)

1094 BEAST (IN A BOX) £250

screenprint
Lucas Croall
(edition of 20 at £100)

1095 PILLS £1,200

gouache on paper
Tom Loffill

1096 HUNTERS IN THE SNOW £245

etching and aquatint
Tim Southall
(edition of 75 at £185)

1097 SELF PORTRAIT AS A BOOK, MAGENTA £450

screenprint
Fiona Banner RA
(edition of 50 at £350)

1098 SELF PORTRAIT AS A BOOK, YELLOW £450

screenprint
Fiona Banner RA
(edition of 50 at £350)

1099 SELF PORTRAIT AS A BOOK, KEY £450

screenprint
Fiona Banner RA
(edition of 50 at £350)

1100 CANDY BROTHERS £778

etching
Giulia Zaniol
(edition of 50 at £678)

1101 IT NEVER EVER STOPS £3,600
acrylic and ink on board
Mariele Neudecker

1102 LIFE IMITATING ART – MY FAVOURITE THINGS £450
etching
Mychael Barratt
(edition of 100 at £350)

1103 OCTOBER MIST £310
etching
Jay Zhang
(edition of 180 at £190)

1104 MANNY £1,500
print on broken marble
Liane Lang
(edition of 5 at £1,400)

1105 BENEATH THE EDGE £400
digital print
Ian Whadcock
(edition of 50 at £200)

1106 MERRY – GO – ROUND £695
lithograph with hand-colouring
Cathie Pilkington RA
(edition of 35 at £550)

1107 GLASS ANIMALS £695
archival digital print with hand-colouring
Cathie Pilkington RA
(edition of 35 at £550)

1108 A–Z £195
photo etching
Kasper Pincis
(edition of 52 at £145)

1109 CAPSULES £470
photo polymer etching
Oscar Lowe
(edition of 25 at £380)

1110 STONE QUARRY 1 £480
chine-collé and photo etching
Tooney Phillips

1111 IT SEEMS WE HAVE DEVELOPED £450
A TASTE FOR EACH OTHER'S WEAKNESSES
photopolymer etching
Pio Abad
(edition of 30 at £350)

1112 THE JOYS OF SIX £695
lithograph with hand-colouring
Cathie Pilkington RA
(edition of 35 at £550)

1113 CYGNUS CYGNUS £695
lithograph with hand-colouring
Cathie Pilkington RA
(edition of 35 at £550)

1114 LITTLE HOUSE ON THE PRAIRIE £650
oil and embroidery thread
Julia Hall

1115 LOVELY EYES £4,500
jesmonite, oil, etching, blanket and lace
Cathie Pilkington RA
(edition of 7 at £4,500)

1116 QUINTESSENCE OF DUST £320
lithograph
Veta Gorner
(edition of 50 at £240)

1117 THUG LIFE £230
linocut
Billie Josef
(edition of 25 at £180)

1118 IDIOT SAVANTS [PALE, MALE AND STALE] £900
screenprint, digital print and hand-colouring
Mark Hampson
(edition of 15 at £750)

1119 ESCAPE FROM PATERSONS LAND £900

pen and gouache
Robbie Bushe

1120 BELL JAR – MARIGOLDS £320

screenprint and laser cut
Chitra Merchant
(edition of 50 at £250)

1121 SHIPWRECK ON INIS OIRR Prints from the edition
available for sale

photography
Michael Collins
(edition of 85 at £240)

1122 UNDERSTANDING NOTHING £900

collage
Maria Rivans

1123 CULLENS PUB REVISITED £385

carborundum on digital print
Leonie King

1124 ANY WHICH WAY £260

linocut
Gail Brodholt
(edition of 75 at £210)

1125 THE EMPTY £7,200

*graphite, silver ink, copper, tarnished-silver leaf
and acrylic on paper*
Hipkiss

1126 LET'S ALL GO DOWN THE BEACH! £349

linocut
Stephen Gibbs
(edition of 69 at £269)

1127 FACE BOOK, A STIRRING BOOK FOR GIRLS £1,500

antique book and ephemera
Alison Stockmarr

1128 NEGOTIATING FREEDOM £190

etching
Sarah Rogers
(edition of 275 at £120)

1129 OVER THE MOUNTAIN £850
woodcut
Sadie Tierney
(edition of 10 at £750)

1130 TOWARDS THE FOREST £235
aquatint
Lucy Ward
(edition of 25 at £195)

1131 INNOCENCE £475
digital photomontage
Simone Riley

1132 DISPERSED COUPLE £500
pencil and collage on Scottish sea pottery
Eve Bridges

1133 AURANIA £1,400
monotype
Alison Lambert

1134 ONE MORNING £225
etching and aquatint
Sonia Martin
(edition of 20 at £175)

1135 VENICE BOAT £740
etching
Dame Elizabeth Blackadder RA
(edition of 40 at £660)

1136 FJORD DRAUMR £850
woodcut
Sadie Tierney
(edition of 10 at £750)

1137 BORDER £180
etching and aquatint
Jane Rollason
(edition of 30 at £150)

1138 TARANSAY MOON WITH FISH AND RICE £280
woodcut
Jonathan Lloyd
(edition of 50 at £220)

1139 PRIAPUS £1,400
monotype
Alison Lambert

1140 PASSAGE OF TIME. VICTORIA STATION £590
drypoint and engraved relief print
Trevor Price
(edition of 75 at £480)

1141 THE ALBATROSS IN THE ROOM £490
photopolymer etching
Pam Aldridge
(edition of 5 at £460)

1142 TYCHE £225
etching
David Huglin
(edition of 50 at £175)

1143 FIRESTONE £370
etching
Martin Langford
(edition of 150 at £310)

1144 COMPASSION NFS
digital collage
John Lawler

1145 L'EQUIPE II £550
inkjet and screenprint
Anthony Green RA
(edition of 25 at £500)

1146 ST JAMES'S SQUARE £875
hand-coloured lithograph
Adam Dant
(edition of 50 at £600)

1147 DOOR DE BOMEN HET BOS NIET MEER £395
KUNNEN ZIEN
lithograph
Fred Robeson
(edition of 50 at £295)

1148 SOUTHERN BELLE £295

screenprint
Lucy Gough
(edition of 50 at £195)

1149 APPLE (LEVITATION) GREEN £2,950

archival inkjet print (in four colour variants)
Langlands & Bell
(edition of 10 at £2,400)

1150 DECEMBER 2017, FINLAND NFS

watercolour and pencil on paper
Caroline Ward-Raatikainen

1151 END OF EMPIRE £350

wood engraving and pochoir
Anne Desmet RA
(edition of 30 at £240)

1152 NO CLEAR SPACE £460

intaglio and block-print
Katherine Jones
(edition of 50 at £375)

1153 BABYLON REBUILT £4,180

*wood engravings and linocut prints on paper
collaged on four ceramic bowls*
Anne Desmet RA

1154 RA METAMORPHOSIS II £335

lithograph
Anne Desmet RA
(edition of 30 at £195)

1155 RA METAMORPHOSIS £335

lithograph
Anne Desmet RA
(edition of 30 at £195)

1156 RA REVOLUTION £630

stone lithograph
Anne Desmet RA
(edition of 35 at £450)

1157 THE RETIREMENT OF THE CHAIRMAN £450

etching
Will Taylor
(edition of 50 at £295)

1158 SAT.I £750

etching
Ian Chamberlain
(edition of 30 at £625)

1159 THE THERAPIST £650

crafted digital pigment print
Nick Greenglass
(edition of 10 at £500)

1160 PADDLING POOL £550

digital print
Geoff Hodgson
(edition of 25 at £500)

1161 STAITH £1,150

screenprint
Mali Morris RA
(edition of 35 at £900)

1162 MAN WITH MIRROR £2,450

from a set of six hard-ground etchings on copper
with aquatint, drypoint and roulette wheel
Paul Noble
(edition of 25 at £2,100)

1163 A LOT OF CASTOR AND POLLUX £875

etching and aquatint
Mick Rooney RA
(edition of 50 at £700)

1164 WOMAN WITH APPLES £2,450

from a set of six hard-ground etchings on copper
with aquatint, drypoint and roulette wheel
Paul Noble
(edition of 25 at £2,100)

1165 ALL THE RIVERS THAT FLOW THROUGH ME £6,450

etching
Mila Furstova
(edition of 18 at £5,750)

1166 TROUBLED WATERS £550

archival inkjet print
Paul Thirkell
(edition of 25 at £495)

1167 BRICK LANE GIRL £250

giclée print
Héloïse Bergman
(edition of 100 at £150)

1168 MYSTERIA £950

linocut
Eileen Cooper RA
(edition of 40 at £800)

1169 CELESTINA £1,100

woodcut
Eileen Cooper RA
(edition of 35 at £950)

1170 INTO THE WAVES £5,000

monotype
Bill Jacklin RA

1171 FALL'D FLABINGO £180

screenprint
Stewart Taylor
(edition of 20 at £130)

1172 WHAT ARE YOUR DREAMS... £400

lithograph
Catherine Ade
(edition of 20 at £325)

1173 TITS FOR TATS £175

block print and ink on vintage book paper
Ceal Warnants
(edition of 100 at £100)

1174	**THROUGH THE VEIL**	£1,800

autostereoscopic lens
Lawrie Hutcheon
(edition of 7 at £1,800)

1175	**900 MIDSUMMER BOULEVARD**	£450

pencil
Emma Wilde

1176	**GLITCH**	£500

giclée print of original Polaroid photograph
Anna-Marie Bush
(edition of 50 at £150)

1177	**ALLÍ (OVER THERE)**	£390

transfer print on Japanese paper
Victoria Ahrens
(edition of 30 at £320)

1178	**BRUTALLY UNTITLED**	£2,500

engraving, monoprint and torn paper
Hector Geoffrey Hamilton

1179	**STARS AND SEA AT NIGHT R**	£7,000

monotype
Bill Jacklin RA

1180	**ANIMALS**	£300

photolithograph
Hannah Jones
(edition of 10 at £200)

1181	**PASSING ACROSS PARLIAMENT HILL**	£570

etching and aquatint
Timothy Hyman RA
(edition of 25 at £420)

1182	**LIBRARY NUDE**	£4,300

archival giclée print
Fiona Banner RA
(edition of 30 at £4,000)

1183	**BLOCKHOUSE**	£550

digital print
Geoff Hodgson
(edition of 25 at £500)

1184 CASSETTE TAPES £355
linocut
Hannah Forward
(edition of 15 at £315)

1185 FEMINIST JUKEBOX £175
giclée print
Pello
(edition of 100 at £125)

1186 ANCIENT COPPICE 1 £750
mixed media
Nik Pollard

1187 AXIS £1,245
screenprint
Paul Huxley RA
(edition of 40 at £995)

1188 MR TURNER'S GRAND DESIGN £400
etching
Marie-Louise Martin
(edition of 50 at £325)

1189 I'M NOT LOST, I'M JUST EXPLORING £850
screenprint
Toby Jury Morgan
(edition of 10 at £600)

1190 MARTIN'S DRAWING PINS £65
relief print on paper and board
Ruth Martin
(edition of 50 at £65)

1191 GABRIEL_RED, BLACK AND BLUE £656
3D polychromatic plaster resin print
Tom Lomax
(edition of 30 at £656)

1192 SINK 1 £1,050
digital print and oil paint on ceramic
Alice Mara

1193 MARTIN'S CULTURE STOCK £70

relief print on paper
Ruth Martin
(edition of 50 at £70)

1194 THIS IS NOT A BRILLO BOX £295

screenprint on acrylic sprayed wooden box and Perspex case
Hayden Kays
(edition of 100 at £295)

1195 TINY SNATCH FANZINE (A TRIBUTE TO THE LIFE £27
AND ART OF LYNDSEY COCKWELL RIP)

paper collage
Emer O'Brien
(edition of 200 at £27)

1196 OBJECT LESSON (ONE) £1,450

inkjet print
Sioban Piercy
(edition of 10 at £1,450)

West

1197 HENGE II £3,000

four colour plate lithograph
Ian McKeever RA
(edition of 25 at £2,700)

1198 HENGE III £3,000

four colour plate lithograph
Ian McKeever RA
(edition of 25 at £2,700)

1199 CAMAS RUBHA A MHURAIN £1,300

screenprint
John Mackechnie
(edition of 20 at £1,100)

1200 KEEL £1,700
archival print on museum etching paper
Subodh Kerkar
(edition of 15 at £1,600)

1201 RAY AT GRANDMAS £180
iPad drawing
Daniel Bonsall
(edition of 100 at £140)

1202 STOLEN THUNDER Prints from the edition
(TWICE REMOVED) available for sale
digital print
Cornelia Parker RA
(edition of 100 at £420)

1203 SPLENDOUR: A DREAM OF THE EASTERN £1,750
CAPITAL_PLUM BLOSSOM SEASON
digital and hand drawing
Freja Lijia Bao

1204 GENTLE MEN HOLD THEIR BREATH £650
photo etching
Adam Hogarth
(edition of 50 at £450)

1205 BETWEEN MAN AND MATTER #2 £2,050
oil-based woodcut
Katsutoshi Yuasa
(edition of 5 at £1,800)

1206 BEFORE THREE £700
archival giclée print
Richard Kirwan
(edition of 30 at £550)

1207 TRACES OF A CHILDHOOD 1 £2,000
monoprint
Susan Aldworth
(edition of 6 at £1,800)

1208 HUMAN CARGO (TRIPTYCH) NFS
conté pencil, conté and ink wash on paper
Dame Paula Rego RA

1209 CARVED PAPER SERIES NO.2 £1,400
oil stick on watercolour paper
Wendy Robin

1210 SLICE £380
screenprint
Emma Lawrenson
(edition of 40 at £290)

1211 PEEP £380
screenprint
Emma Lawrenson
(edition of 40 at £290)

1212 A DEBACLE. WHIRLIGIGS VERSUS HUMAN £1,050
FLIES. ICE CREAM ANGELS DISPENSE
HEALING BALM. MALICIOUS IMPS LICK
THE SOLES OF THE DISHEARTENED
digital print
Kevin O'Keefe
(edition of 25 at £850)

1213 LINEAS ON GREEN £400
pigment print
Ana Ayesta
(edition of 30 at £300)

1214 LESSON 1 £750
monotype
Stephen Snoddy

1215 SWAN (BLUE) £4,800
archival giclée print
Hugh Hamshaw-Thomas
(edition of 5 at £4,000)

1216 NORTHERN LIGHT £2,250
woodcut
Pine Feroda
(edition of 60 at £1,950)

1217 CATO WORDS POST 14.12.2010 £400
monotype
Emma Douglas

1218 WALK AMONG DRAGONFLIES £210
etching
Ralph Overill
(edition of 24 at £170)

1219 MANHATTAN SERIES: MOMENTS IN TIME £4,500
(from left to right: Sun, Twilight, Stars,
Night Becomes Day, Sky, Rain, Storm,
Snow, Snow on Snow)
wood engraving, linocut and stencilling
Anne Desmet RA
(edition of 20, with the exception of Sky, which is
an edition of 30, at £3,150 for the series)

1220 HIGH FALLS 1 £800
woodcut
Rod Nelson
(edition of 50 at £650)

1221 FLIP SIDE £1,500
screenprint
Frea Buckler

1222 INTO THE BLACK £2,200
woodcut on Japanese Misumi paper
Christiane Baumgartner
(edition of 30 at £1,900)

1223 DESIGN FOR A CAKE BASKET AND TWO £5,700
MUFFINEERS EN-SUITE I
etching hand-coloured with lemon yellow ink
Pablo Bronstein
(edition of 30 at £5,100)

1224 STILL LIFE WITH KIDNEY STONE £220
photo etching
Peter Doubleday
(edition of 20 at £130)

1225 MOTHER 6 WE ALWAYS KNEW YOU £22,000
hand-painted lithograph
Tracey Emin RA

1226 MOTHER 3 A WAY OF LEAVING £22,000
hand-painted lithograph
Tracey Emin RA

1227 GASCONADE, BURNSLOW £840
digital print
Mat Collishaw
(edition of 75 at £660)

1228 GASCONADE, BEASTMODE £840
digital print
Mat Collishaw
(edition of 75 at £660)

1229 EARLY MORNING £9,000
reduction woodcut
Tom Hammick
(edition of 9 at £8,000)

1230 SAYING GOODBYE £1,250
polymer gravure
Tracey Emin RA
(edition of 100 at £850)

1231 BIRD ON A WING AFTER DB £1,100
polymer gravure
Tracey Emin RA
(edition of 200 at £575)

1232 GREEN FAÇADE £650
ink
Rika Newcombe

1233 TEA 42 NFS
collage
Stephanie Franks

1234 HEALERS £2,775
etching
Kiki Smith HON RA
(edition of 24)

1235 CREST #3 £280
cyanotype
Helen Dixon
(edition of 30 at £180)

1236 LENIN'S SCIENCE MAKES ONE'S HANDS AND MIND STRONGER £4,200
bromoil on silver gelatin paper
Gregori Maiofis
(edition of 25 at £4,200)

1237 FUNT WITH HARP £12,500
bromoil transfer on Yupo paper
Gregori Maiofis
(edition of 5 at £12,500)

1238 MATRIX III £2,400
aquatint from multiple plates
Antony Gormley RA
(edition of 25 at £2,150)

1239 MATRIX I £2,400
aquatint from multiple plates
Antony Gormley RA
(edition of 25 at £2,150)

1240 MATRIX II £2,400
aquatint from multiple plates
Antony Gormley RA
(edition of 25 at £2,150)

1241 BORDER WALL £450
archival pigment print
Richard Wilson RA
(edition of 30 at £400)

1242 ETON COLLEGE LIBRARY AND SHE IV £1,600
archival pigment print
Guler Ates
(edition of 15 at £1,250)

1243 WIRED / WIRELESS £2,450
from a series of letterpress prints
Sir Michael Craig-Martin RA
(edition of 20 at £2,100)

1244 CHANGING LIGHT 2 £2,820
hand-made woodcut
Christopher Le Brun PRA
(edition of 12 at £2,400)

1245	**CHANGING LIGHT 1**	£2,820
	hand-made woodcut	
	Christopher Le Brun PRA	
	(edition of 12 at £2,400)	

1246	**CHANGING LIGHT 4**	£2,820
	hand-made woodcut	
	Christopher Le Brun PRA	
	(edition of 12 at £2,400)	

1247	**CHANGING LIGHT 3**	£2,820
	hand-made woodcut	
	Christopher Le Brun PRA	
	(edition of 12 at £2,400)	

1248	**LATE AFTERNOON**	£700
	screenprint	
	Clare Cutts	
	(edition of 20 at £525)	

1249	**CASSETTE / SPOTIFY**	£2,450
	from a series of letterpress prints	
	Sir Michael Craig-Martin RA	
	(edition of 20 at £2,100)	

1250	**FEARFUL SYMMETRY**	£800
	aquatint	
	Peter Freeth RA	
	(edition of 30 at £650)	

1251	**IN THE FOREST OF THE NIGHT**	£800
	aquatint	
	Peter Freeth RA	
	(edition of 30 at £650)	

1252	**THIS IS TOMORROW, TODAY II**	£600
	stone lithograph, monoprint and collage	
	Mandy Payne	
	(edition of 16 at £500)	

1253	**THE LIGHT HOUSE**	£380
	woodcut	
	Chun-Chao Chiu	
	(edition of 5 at £300)	

1254 TRANSATLANTIC FLIGHT £300
aquatint
Michael O'Mahony
(edition of 50 at £200)

1255 RIVER BANK £550
aquatint
Peter Freeth RA
(edition of 30 at £450)

1256 CHARGER £700
screenprint
Zsofia Schweger
(edition of 35 at £580)

1257 IN THE MOUNTAINS 2 £600
archival digital print
Jane Ward
(edition of 30 at £500)

1258 BLIND LANDING, LAB 5, H-BOMB TEST £26,000
FACILITY, ORFORD NESS, SUFFOLK
c-type print on aluminium with Diasec
Jane & Louise Wilson RA
(edition of 4 at £26,000)

1259 TAKING THE PLUNGE £550
aquatint
Peter Freeth RA
(edition of 40 at £450)

1260 MR PARKINSON LISTENS TO THE BIRDSONG £550
aquatint
Peter Freeth RA
(edition of 40 at £450)

1261 MR P TO THE RESCUE £550
aquatint
Peter Freeth RA
(edition of 30 at £450)

1262 TATE SHADOW WAITING £650
photopolymer gravure
Simon Lawson
(edition of 50 at £450)

1263 KIYEMBE LANE £950

hand-coloured etching
Bronwen Sleigh
(edition of 25 at £800)

1264 MOVE IT £2,000

inkjet and screenprint
Allen Jones RA
(edition of 40 at £2,000)

1265 ONE GRAIN OF RICE £9,500

interactive steel, wood and rice construction
Tim Lewis

1266 MAN FALLS £470

archival inkjet print with two-colour screenprint overlay
Charming Baker
(edition of 125 at £295)

1267 FUEL PUMP £750

c-type print
Michael Rudman
(edition of 20 at £600)

1268 POLRIDMOUTH COAST £6,800

*from a series of four digital prints float mounted
onto glass and presented in artist's frames*
Julian Opie
(edition of 20 at £6,800)

1269 DIMINISH 1 £750

etching
Jo Gorner
(edition of 30 at £600)

1270 TOWER, DAYTON WA £7,500

archival pigment print
Boyd & Evans
(edition of 5 at £6,650)

1271 VERDWENEN STAD. MOMENTS. I £425

lithography
Malgorzata Olchowska
(edition of 7 at £325)

1272 FARO £480

monoprint

Sarah Granville

1273 FOUNTAIN £1,100

letterpress

Alan Kitching

(edition of 12 at £825)

1274 TOWER, CHERRY CREEK NV £7,500

archival pigment print

Boyd & Evans

(edition of 5 at £6,650)

1275 ART SCHOOL II £2,900

from a series of eight polymer photogravures with woodblock

Paul Winstanley

(edition of 12 at £2,600)

1276 YOUNG ACADEMICIAN £138,000

fibreglass mannequin, Dutch wax printed cotton textile, books,
globe and steel baseplate

Yinka Shonibare RA

1277 CROCODILE HEAD £8,950

bronze

James Mortimer

(edition of 9)

McAulay Gallery

1278 GANGLAND CAFF — NFS
menu board
Andrew Lee

1279 CHRISTINA TAKES ALAN MEASLES FOR TEA AT JULIE'S HOUSE — £300
oil
Susan Donnelly

1280 MOST ADVANCED. YET ACCEPTABLE — £5
linocut and digital print
Maya Heathcote

1281 MEIN — £240
acrylic
Nicola Clark

1282 I LOVE ALAN — £500
name tapes and dressmaker pins on canvas
Joy Pitts

1283 BRITISH ARTISTS SERIES #2 — £350
knitted wool
Rod Melvin

1284 HOPONN — £775
giclée print
Luke Stephenson
(edition of 10 at £600)

1285 THE LOVE OF GRAYSON — £450
acrylic
Cynthia Underdown

1286 GRAYSON PERRY...YOU SHOULD HAVE GONE TO SPECSAVERS — £950
acrylic
Rodney Holt

1287 GRAYSON CLAIRE WITH CAT AND BEAR £500
acrylic
Diana Poliak

1288 GRAYSON £2,500
oil
Jean Samtula

1289 SUCKING UP TO GRAYSON £1,400
oil
Hannah Flinders

1290 I LOVE CLAIRE £500
name tapes and dressmaker pins on canvas
Joy Pitts

1291 ANDY WARHOL IN DRAG (5) £10,500
oil on wood
Annie Kevans

1292 SELLFRIDGES £225
c-type print
Patrick Dalton
(edition of 151 at £75)

1293 UNCOUTH ROAD, MILNROW £175
giclée print
Dominic Greyer
(edition of 150 at £95)

1294 SNOW WHITE THE SCIENTIST £290
archival inkjet print
Sarah Maple
(edition of 50 at £175)

1295 CUMCUM HILL, HERTFORDSHIRE £175
giclée print
Dominic Greyer
(edition of 150 at £95)

1296 UNTITLED £5,400
poster pen and screenprint on paper
David Shrigley

1297 UNTITLED £5,400

poster pen and screenprint on paper
David Shrigley

1298 UNTITLED £5,400

poster pen and screenprint on paper
David Shrigley

1299 UNTITLED £5,400

poster pen and screenprint on paper
David Shrigley

1300 UNTITLED £5,400

poster pen and screenprint on paper
David Shrigley

1301 UNTITLED £5,400

poster pen and screenprint on paper
David Shrigley

1302 UNTITLED £5,400

poster pen and screenprint on paper
David Shrigley

1303 UNTITLED £5,400

poster pen and screenprint on paper
David Shrigley

1304 UNTITLED £5,400

poster pen and screenprint on paper
David Shrigley

1305 UNTITLED £5,400

poster pen and screenprint on paper
David Shrigley

1306 UNTITLED £5,400

poster pen and screenprint on paper
David Shrigley

1307 UNTITLED £5,400

poster pen and screenprint on paper
David Shrigley

1308 UNTITLED £5,400

poster pen and screenprint on paper
David Shrigley

1309	**UNTITLED**	£5,400
	poster pen and screenprint on paper	
	David Shrigley	
1310	**UNTITLED**	£5,400
	poster pen and screenprint on paper	
	David Shrigley	
1311	**UNTITLED**	£5,400
	poster pen and screenprint on paper	
	David Shrigley	
1312	**UNTITLED**	£5,400
	poster pen and screenprint on paper	
	David Shrigley	
1313	**UNTITLED**	£5,400
	poster pen and screenprint on paper	
	David Shrigley	
1314	**UNTITLED**	£5,400
	poster pen and screenprint on paper	
	David Shrigley	
1315	**UNTITLED**	£5,400
	poster pen and screenprint on paper	
	David Shrigley	
1316	**SUMMER EXHIBITION 2016**	£1,250
	oil	
	Jacob Brown	
1317	**LONELINESS. 'TO FEEL ALONE IN A ROOM FULL OF PEOPLE'**	£1,495
	oil on linen	
	Peter Allwright	
1318	**LOWRY FIGURES VISITING A DAMIEN HIRST EXHIBITION**	£130
	felt tip pen and cellophane	
	Jonathan Hajdamach	
1319	**PORTRAIT OF THE ARTIST AT HIS SOLO EXHIBITION**	£1,200
	mixed media	
	Blake O'Donnell	

1320 BOTANICAL GARDENS, OOTY, INDIA £4,950

pigment print
Martin Parr
(edition of 10 at £4,800)

1321 BAGA BEACH, GOA, INDIA £4,950

pigment print
Martin Parr
(edition of 10 at £4,800)

1322 BAGA BEACH, GOA, INDIA £4,950

pigment print
Martin Parr
(edition of 10 at £4,800)

1323 OUR LADY OF THE IMMACULATE CONCEPTION £4,950
CHURCH, PANAJIM, GOA, INDIA

pigment print
Martin Parr
(edition of 10 at £4,800)

1324 CHOWPATTY BEACH, MUMBAI, INDIA £4,950

pigment print
Martin Parr
(edition of 10 at £4,800)

1325 MYSORE ZOO, INDIA £4,950

pigment print
Martin Parr
(edition of 10 at £4,800)

1326 ANOTHER FINE MESS YOU'VE GOT US INTO £250

frosted Perspex and transparency film on light box
Guy Morris

1327 AMERICAN DREAM CAKE STAND £1,000

ceramic
Carol Mcnicoll

1328 TRANSVESTITE SELFIE £5,000

polymer clay
Wilfrid Wood

1329 CLAIRE HAS MEASLES £600

cotton fabric, acrylic and wax
Sue Hurman

1330 VENUS CHRIST, MORNING STAR £6,200
enamel paint and gold leaf on jesmonite
Jamie Clements
(edition of 3 at £6,200)

1331 YOUNGER, HIPPER, COOLER £1,000
mixed media
Rosie Raven

1332 MY LAST ROLO £3,500
bronze, 9 carat gold, silver plate and acrylic oil paint
Jane Morgan
(edition of 10 at £3,500)

1333 DELAYED REACTIONS - FROWNING FACE NFS
lapis lazuli and gold
Lin Cheung

1334 SOMETHING FOR THE WEEKEND £700
concrete and car wax
Alexandra Searle

1335 BOOKAXE £11,000
bronze
Peter Clay
(edition of 5 at £11,000)

1336 GRAYSON PERRY BURIAL URN £595
glazed ceramic
Laina Watt

1337 CALL ME CLAIRE £450
clay and acrylic
Aimee Morris

1338 RAY RINKOFF NFS
MDF, acrylic and 3D print
Acrylicize

**1339 ODE TO KITSCH AND POP ART
(TABLE DECORATION PIECE)** NFS
clay
Jane Welch
(edition of 2)

1340 THE UNBEARABLE LIGHTNESS OF SEEING   £1,000
ceramic, aluminium and bronze powder, glue, paint, polish and metal clamp with bar
Kay Latto

1341 TRUNKS II   £1,600
wood, gloss paint, steel threaded rod and dome nuts
Jason Brown

1342 BLUE AND WHITE PORCELAIN   Sculpture from the edition
porcelain   available for sale
Zhang Songtao
(edition of 10 at £400)

1343 SPACED (VERSION 2)   £8,300
fibreglass, polyester filler, 2k paint and acrylic
Garry Martin

1344 CLOSING DOWN SALE   £42,000
mixed media and audio
Michael Landy RA

1345 TULIPS   £96,000
painted bronze
Gavin Turk

1346 FLAG WAVER   £7,000
steel, motor, pulleys and flag
Nik Ramage

1347 GREEN LEAF GATED   £120,000
painted foam PVC and polyurethane foam
Phillip King PPRA

Wohl
Entrance Hall

1348 THIRTEEN DAYS WALKING ON DARTMOOR   *
text work
Sir Richard Long RA

1349 DAYMARK £92,000
syenite
John Maine RA

1350 TURNING POINT £46,000
gneiss
John Maine RA

1351 CYCLADIC GEMINI £300,000
Egyptian alabaster
Stephen Cox RA

The Great Spectacle

Gallery I

1352 ALWAYS ALMOST NFS
Oil on canvas
Christopher Le Brun PRA

Refer to sales desk.

List of Exhibitors

A

Abad, Pio, Gasworks, 155 Vauxhall Street, London SE11 5RH, **1111**

Abele, Julia, Lutherstraße 1, Heidelberg, Baden-würtemberg, 69120, Germany **212**

ABRAMOVIĆ, Marina, HON RA, Courtesy of Lisson Gallery, **756**

ACKROYD, Prof. Noman, CBE RA, 1 Morocco Street, London SE1 3HB, **915, 919, 920, 921, 923, 924**

Ackroyd & Harvey, Studio 9, North Street, Dorking RH4 1DN, **749, 1008**

Acrylicize, c/o James Burke, 1A Old Nichol Street, London E2 7HR, **1338**

Adam, Thomas, 64 Firs Close, London SE23 1BB, **932**

Adam Khan Architects and muf architecture/art, 45 Vyner Street, London E2 9DQ, **660**

Ade, Catherine, 27 Grasmere Close, Westbury on Trym, Bristol BS10 6AU, **1172**

Adela, Renata, 7A St Marks Crescent, London NW1 7TS, **266**

Adesina, Ade, 8 Bethany House, Bethany Garden, Aberdeen AB11 6YD, **477**

ADJAYE, Sir David, OBE RA, Adjaye Associates, The Edison, 223–231 Old Marylebone Road, London NW1 5QT, **667**

Agenjo, David, Studio 1, Unit 4, Ravensdale Industrial Estate, Timberwharf Road, London N16 6DB, **213**

AHR/PCKO, 5–8 Hardwick Street, London EC1R 4RG, **677**

Ahrens, Victoria, Flat 7, Mural House, 5A Havil Street, London SE5 7FS, **992, 1177**

Ainslie, Prudence, 9 Fairfield Road, London E3 2QA, **1082**

AKT II, White Collar Factory, 1 Old Street Yard, London EC1Y 8AF, **609, 653**

AL_A, 14A Brewery Road, London N7 9NH, **607**

Alalba, Ana, 92 Tollington Park, London N4 3RB, **1036**

Alan-Kidd, Michael, 11 Danemere Street, Putney, London SW15 1LT, **33**

Albert, c/o Bethlem Gallery, Bethlem Royal Hospital, Monks Orchard Road, Beckenham, Kent BR3 3BX, **268**

Aldridge, Pam, 138 Crescent Drive South, Woodingdean, Brighton BN2 6SA, **1141**

Aldworth, Susan, c/o TAG Fine Arts, Unit 129A Business Design Centre, 52 Upper Street, London N1 0QH, **1207**

Alexander, Naomi, 6 The Bishops Avenue, London N2 0AN, **230**

Alexander, Mark, c/o Mark Glatman, Well Hall, Bedale Road, Well, Bedale, Yorkshire DL8 2PX, **335**

Aliaga, Maxime, Marsh View, Friars Lane Burnham Norton, King's Lynn, Norfolk PE31 8JA, **172**

Alison Brooks Architects, Unit 610 Highgate Studios, 53-79 Highgate Road, London NW5 1TL, **662**

Allan, Nicholas, Flat D, 40A Walnut Tree Walk, London SE11 6DN, **709**

Allchurch, Emily, 3 Chapel Mews, Marianne Park, Old London Road, Hastings TN35 5PS, **1002**

Allen, Ambrosine, 16 Croftongate Way, London SE4 2DL, **439, 499**

Allos, Liana, Oakridge, 106 Queens Road, Walton on Thames KT12 5LL, **950**

Allwright, Peter, 10 Lancaster Road, Goring-by-Sea, Worthing, West Sussex BN12 4BP, **1317**

alma-nac, 11 Waterloo Court, 10 Theed Street, London SE1 8ST, **596**

Alsop, Piers, Flat D, 1 Heyworth Road, London E5 8DR, **125**

ALSOP, the late Prof. Will, OBE RA, All Design, 1-5 Vyner Street, London E2 9DG, **513, 519, 520, 588**

Analts, Arthur, 374 Old Street, London EC1V 9LT, **487**

ANATSUI, El, HON RA, Courtesy of October Gallery, 24 Old Gloucester Street, London WC1N 3AL, **696**

Anderson, Raymond, c/o Bethlem Gallery, Bethlem Royal Hospital, Monks Orchard Road, Beckenham, Kent BR3 3BX, **851**

Anderson, Sandi, 30 Kelvinside Gardens, Glasgow G20 6BB, **1048**

Ansell, Amanda, 3 St Andrews Road, Great Cornard, Sudbury, Suffolk CO10 0DB, **106**

Antoni Malinowski & Fenella Collingridge, 19 Penn Road, London N7 9RD, **597**

Appleby, Jemma, Burwood, Southill Road, Chislehurst, Kent BR7 5EE, **816, 817**

ARAD, Ron, RA, Ron Arad Associates, 62 Chalk Farm Road, London NW1 8AN, **678, 679, 680, 681**

Archer, Magda, c/o John Ash, Pew Literary, 46 Lexington Street, London W1F 0LP, **17, 349**

Architectural Advice, c/o Malcolm Dickson, Architectural Advice, 6 Fletcher House, 122 Nuttall Street, London N1 5LL, **575**

Architecture 00, 64 Skinners Lane, London KT21 2LY, **621**

Armah, Lucy, 7 Templar Street, London SE5 9JB, **1081**

ARMFIELD, Diana, RA, Courtesy of Chris Beetles Gallery, 8 & 10 Ryder Street, London SW1Y 6QB, **61, 94, 121, 267, 311, 314**

Armstrong, Joseph, Apartment 16, Westminster Bridge House, 6 Lambeth Road, London SE1 6HT, **812**

Armstrong-Jones, Sarah, Courtesy of The Redfern Gallery, 20 Cork Street, London SW1 3HL, **368, 369**

BARLOW, Prof. Phyllida, CBE RA, Courtesy of Hauser & Wirth, 23 Savile Row, London W1S 2ET, **740**

Barrall, Martin, 42 Newton Drive, Sawbridgeworth, Hertfordshire CM21 9HE, **127**

Barratt, Mychael, 18 Birchwood Avenue, London N10 3BE, **1102**

Barrington, c/o Bethlem Gallery, Bethlem Royal Hospital, Monks Orchard Road, Beckenham, Kent BR3 3BX, **6**

Batchelor, David, Brickfield Studios, Brickfield Road (off Empson Street), London E3 3LT, **329**

Bateman, Henry, 33 Latimer Road, London E7 0LQ, **351**

Baumgartner, Christiane, Courtesy of Alan Cristea Gallery, 43 Pall Mall, London SW1Y 5JG, **1222**

Baxter, Glen, c/o Flowers Gallery, 82 Kingsland Road, London E2 8DP, **274**

Beach, Patricia, 7 Reservoir Road, Ladywood, Birmingham B16 9EL, **109**

Beales, David, c/o Bethlem Gallery, Bethlem Royal Hospital, Monks Orchard Road, Beckenham, Kent BR3 3BX, **34**

BEATTIE, Basil, RA, 1 Village School House, Lower Green West, Mitcham, Surrey CR4 3AF, **176, 388, 855**, Courtesy of Advanced Graphics London 68 Walcot Square, London SE11 4TZ, **970**

Beattie, Dominic, 1B Boone Street, London SE13 5SD, **820**

Beesley, Mark, 45 Old Barrack Road, Woodbridge, Suffolk IP12 4ET, **1091**

Begum, Rana, **824**

Bell-Salter, Elfia, 6 York Terrace West, London NW1 4QA, **22**

Belous, Anastasia, 2 Connaught Mansions, Prince of Wales Drive, London SW11 4SA, **199**

Ben Terrett & Russell Davies, 105 Holcroft Court, Clipstone Street, London W1W 5DH, **66**

Bennett, Jonathan, 11 Graham Road, London E8 1DA, **272**

Bennetts Associates Architects, c/o Elizabeth Walker, 1 Rawstorne Place, London EC1V 7NL, **581, 625**

Benson, Amanda, 38 Milfields Road, London E5 0SB, **882**

BENSON, Prof. Gordon, OBE RA, 40 Charlton Kings Road, London NW5 2SA, **545, 546, 547, 548, 549, 550**

Bergman, Héloïse, 60B Elizabeth Avenue, London N1 3BH, **1167**

Bernstein, Keith, 48 Surrenden Crescent, Brighton BN1 6WF, **108**

Berrington, James, 30 Netherby Road, London SE23 3AN, **366**

BEVAN, Tony, RA, c/o Ben Brown Fine Arts, 12 Brook's Mews, London W1K 4DG, **181**

Bharwani, Jyoti, PaintSpaces Studio, 167 Broadhurst Gardens, London NW6 3AU, **841**

Birds Portchmouth Russum Architects Ltd, Unit 11, Union Wharf, 23 Wenlock Road, London N1 7SB, **553**, **595**

BLACKADDER, Dame Elizabeth, DBE RA, Courtesy of Glasgow Print Studio, 103 Trongate, Glasgow, G1 5HD, **997**, **998**, **1135**

Blackhall, Amy-Jane, 25 Gastard Lane, Gastard, Corsham, Wiltshire SN13 9QP, **497**, **498**

Blackmore, Tony, Flat 2, 7 Gainsford Road, London E17 6QB, **808**

Blake, Helen G., Cleavers Cottage, Carmel Street, Great Chesterford, Essex CB10 1PH, **219**

Blewitt, Timothy, 29 Harvey Road, Goring-by-Sea, Worthing, West Sussex BN12 4DS, **502**, **509**

Bliss, Camilla, 4 Tanza Road, London NW3 2UB, **32**

Bloom, Phillipa, 24 Siu Hang Hau Village, Clear Water Bay, New Territories, Hong Kong, **728**

Bloomfield, Matthew, 84B Mountgrove Road, London N5 2LT, **525**

Blunt, Susanna, 1573 Bowser Avenue, Vancouver BC, V7P 2Y4, Canada **456**, **457**

Boletsi, Angeliki, 26A Cambridge Road, Hove, East Sussex BN3 1DF, **449**

Bonsall, Daniel, Flat 5, 2 Belfield Road, Didsbury, Manchester M20 6BH, **1201**

Bot, G. W., c/o Rebecca Hossack Gallery, 28 Charlotte Street, London W1T 2NA, **1040**, **1051**

Bousfield, Neil, c/o Inky Fingers Press, Lokeside Cottage, Common Road, Hempstead, Norfolk NR12 0DQ, **1088**, **1089**

Bowcott, Marcus, 1347 Oakwood Crescent, North Vancouver, V7P 1L6, Canada, **445**

BOWEY, Olwyn, RA, Random Cottage, Peace Lane, Heyshott, Midhurst, West Sussex GU29 0DF, **112**, **183**

BOWLING, Frank, OBE RA, Courtesy of Hales Gallery, 7 Bethnal Green Road, London E1 6LA, **19**, **87**, **286**

Bowman, Michael, 7 Westgate Road, Beckenham BR3 5DT, **916**

Boyd, Louisa, Fullersmoor Cottage, Smithy Lane, Brown Knowl, Broxton, Chester CH3 9JY, **938**

Boyd & Evans, c/o Flowers Gallery, 82 Kingsland Road, London E2 8DP, **1270**, **1274**

Brady Mallalieu Architects Ltd, Studio D, 400 Caledonian Road, London N1 1DN, **576**, **578**

Bray, David, 4 Dawsons Cottages, The Green, West Farleigh, Kent ME15 0NN, **986**

Bridges, Eve, 19 Glossop Road, Hayfield, High Peak, Derbyshire SK22 2NF, **1132**

Broadbent, Tom, 48 Braidwood Road, London SE6 1QX, **303**

Brodholt, Gail, Studio TB/24, Thames-side Studios, Harrington Way, London SE18 5NR, **1124**

Bronson, Bethe, 4 Manor Cottages Approach, London N2 8JR, **979**

Bronstein, Pablo, Courtesy of Alan Cristea Gallery, 43 Pall Mall, London SW1Y 5JG, **1223**

Brown, Jackie, 20A Westwood Park, Forest Hill, London SE23 3QF, **809**

Brown, Jacob, 4 Nicolson Square, Edinburgh EH8 9BH, **1316**

Brown, Jason, G12 BV Studios, 37 Philip Street, Bedminster, Bristol BS3 4EA, **1341**

Buckler, Frea, 36 Shaldon Road, Bristol BS7 9NW, **1037, 1221**

Bull, Johnny, 12 Chaldicotts Barns, Semley, Shaftesbury, Wiltshire SP7 9AW, **426**

Bullock, Ross, Flat 2-4, 19 King Henrys Road, London NW3 3QP, **901**

Bumbum, Malou, Grebbestraat 34, The Hague, 2515 VV D, Netherlands, **148**

Buonaguidi, Dave, c/o Jealous Gallery, 53 Curtain Road, London EC2A 3PT, **971**

Burdiak, Jane, 49 Willen Road, Newport Pagnell, Buckinghamshire MK16 ODE, **751, 780**

Bureau de Change Architects, Studio 3, 18 Coronet Street, London N1 6HD, **613**

Burke, James, Unit 5, Robert Eliot Center, 1A Old Nichol Street, London E2 7HR, **400**

Burrough, Tim, 74 Camberwell Church Street, London SE5 8QZ, **738**

Burrows, Linda, 17 Albert Mansions, Albert Bridge Road, London SW11 4QB, **315**

Burt, Amy, Flat 1, 31 Montague Road, London E8 2HN, **139**

Busch, Rachel, 32 Cleveland Avenue, London W4 1SN, **1038**

Bush, Thomas, 3 Press Lane, Norwich NR3 2JY, **633**

Bush, Anna-Marie, 20 Albion Street, Chipping Norton, Oxfordshire OX7 5BJ, **1176**

Bushe, Robbie, 3 Oxgangs Farm Drive, Edinburgh EH13 9QH, **1119**

BUTLER, James, MBE RA, Courtesy of Chris Beetles Gallery, 8 & 10 Ryder Street, London SW1Y 6QB, **9, 506, 508, 785, 788, 791**

Butterworth, Jon, 166 Kings Road, Harrow, Middlesex, HA2 9JH, **935**

Byrne, Celie, Dullomuir House, Blairadam, Kelty, Fife KY4 0JG, **425**

Byrne, Julie, 35E Street NW, Apartment 310, Washington, DC, United States **187**

Byrne, Philip, 121 Park Hill, London SW4 9NX, **494**

C

Camilo, Julian, 12 Holmwood Grove, London NW7 3DT, **974**

CAMP, Jeffery, RA, Courtesy of Art Space Gallery, 84 St Peter's Street, London N1 8JS, **136, 278, 285, 313**

Campbell, Gavin Iain, 4 St Andrews Croft, Alwoodley, Leeds LS17 7TP, **931**

Camps, Lorsen, 15 Stamford Avenue, Coventry CV3 5BW, **702**

Cardwell, Jon, Flat 3, 34 Pepys Road, London SE14 5SB, **911**

Carl Turner Architects & Jan Kattein Architects, Unit 61 Regent Studios, 8 Andrews Road, London E8 4QN, **526**

Carlon, Zoe, 59 Oakenshaw Lane, Walton, Wakefield WF2 6NJ, **691**

Carmody Groarke, 62-70 Shorts Gardens, London WC2H 9AH, **584**

Carpanini, David L., Fernlea, 145 Rugby Road, Milverton, Leamington Spa, Warwickshire CV32 6DJ, **934**

Carter, Andrew, 44 Landells Road, London SE22 9PQ, **1065**

CARTER, John, RA, Courtesy of The Redfern Gallery, 20 Cork Street, London W1S 3HL, **194, 209, 850, 852**

Carter, Rob and Nick, 5A Bathurst Street, London W2 2SD, **465, 736**

Cary, Caroline, Avenida de Andalucia 14, Murchas, Granada 18656, Spain **831**

Cary, Samantha, 19 Castle Drive, Berwick-upon-Tweed TD15 1NS, **1059**

Catherall, Paul, 137 Bouverie Road, London N16 0AA, **1068**

CATLING, Prof. Brian, RA, 19 Arthur Street, Oxford OX2 0AS, **763, 770, 847**

Cattlin, Jane, Flagstones, Brooks Green Road, Coolham, Horsham, West Sussex RH13 8GR, **235**

Cavanaugh, Sean, 315 West 39th Street, 1200 New York, NY 10018, United States **705**

Cembrowicz, Cordelia, 724 Holmefield House, Hazlewood Crescent, London W10 5FU, **495**

Chamberlain, Ian, 43 Irby Road, Ashton, Bristol BS3 2LZ, **1158**

Chambers, Catherine, 10 Kings Way, Harrow HA1 1XU, **114**

Chambers, Charles, 78 Paramount Court, University Street, London WC1E 6JW, **1041**

CHAMBERS, Stephen, RA, Stephen Chambers Studio Ltd, (rear of) 7 Clapton Square, London E5 8HP, **103, 1016, 1017, 1018, 1019, 1020**

Chang, Won Young, Flat 54, Horton House, Field Road, London W6 8HW, **451**

Chappell, Lisa, 194 Fortis Green Road, London N10 3DU, **917**

Chetwood, Laurie, Chetwoods, 12-13 Clerkenwell Green, London EC1R 0QJ, **517, 518**

Cheung, Lin, **1333**

Cheung, Gordon, Courtesy of Alan Cristea Gallery, 43 Pall Mall, London SW1Y 5JG, **1070**

Chisholm, Elizabeth, 10 Havelock Walk, London SE23 3HG, **467**

Chiu, Chun-Chao, 31 Church Lane, Newcastle upon Tyne NE3 1AR, **1253**

CHRISTOPHER, Ann, RA, The Stable Block, Hay Street, Marshfield, Chippenham, Wiltshire SN14 8PF, **748, 762, 821**

Chuah, Chong Yan, Flat 24, 27 Central Square, St Marks Street, London E1 8EF, **535**

Chung, Sooyoung, Flat 969, Aquarius House, 15 St Georges Wharf, London SW8 2FD, **484**

Clark, Nicola, 2 New Cottages, Wasperton, Warwick CV35 8EB, **1281**

Clarke, Jim, Flat B, 187 Blackstock Road, London N5 2LL, **755**

Clarkson, Jenny, 58 Vernon Street, Lincoln LN5 7QT, **468**

Clay, Peter, 12 Apsley Way, Longthorpe, Peterborough PE3 9NE, **1335**

Clear, Nic, Unit 4, 98 De Beauvoir Road, London N1 4EN, **646**

Clements, Jamie, Pequod, 23 Blacklands Lane, Sudbourne IP12 2AX, **1330**

Clutterbuck, Esmé, 40 Eldon Terrace, Windmill Hill, Bristol BS3 4PA, **1001**

Cockburn, Julie, c/o Flowers Gallery, 82 Kingsland Road, London E2 8DP, **1042, 1046**

Collett, Ruth, 4 Oaksey Grove, Nailsea, North Somerset BS48 2TP, **458**

Collin, Ashley, Flat 2, 27 Thornbury Court, Southampton SO15 5BQ, **357**

Collins, Michael, 155 Oakcourt Drive, Palmerstown, Dublin 20, **1121**

Collishaw, Mat, c/o Paul Stolper Gallery, 31 Museum Street, London WC1A 1LH, **1227, 1228**

Colussi, Francesca, 24 St Hilary's Drive, Deganwy, Conwy LL31 9SS, **231, 257**

Constable, Sarah, Quires, Brewers Hill, Sandgate, Folkestone, Kent CT20 3DH, **378**

COOK, Prof. Sir Peter, RA, Crab Studio, 81 Essex Road, London N1 2SF, **555, 559, 567, 568, 622**

COOPER, Eileen, OBE RA, 10 Darling Road, London SE4 1YQ, **874, 1031, 1168, 1169**

Coutts, Marion, 43 Spenser Road, London SE24 0NS, **330**

Coverca, Elena Alina, 71 Orchard Road, Southsea, Portsmouth PO4 0AA, **225**

Cox, Don, 27 Canon Close, Rochester, Kent ME1 3EN, **218**

Cox, Martin, 7 Richmond Avenue, London N1 0NE, **227**

COX, Stephen, RA, Lower House Farm, Coreley, Nr Ludlow, Shropshire SY8 3AS, **5**, **886**, **887**, **1351**

Coy, Stuart, 37 Ash Road, Lower Hacheston, Suffolk IP13 0PB, **1029**

CRAGG, Prof. Sir Tony, CBE RA, c/o Royal Academy of Arts, London **729**, **730**

CRAIG-MARTIN, Sir Michael, CBE RA, Courtesy the artist, Gagosian Gallery, **247**, **292**, Courtesy of Alan Cristea Gallery, 43 Pall Mall, London SW1Y 5JG, **1009**, **1010**, **1243**, **1249**

Creenaune, Danielle, Calle Pons i Gallarza 25, pis 2, Barcelona, Catalunya, 8030, Spain, **1033**

Crisp, Yolanda, 6 Pembroke Road, London E17 9PB, **177**

Crispin Kelly & Salter+Collingridge, 71 Queensway, London W2 4QH, **661**

Croall, Lucas, 14 Iliffe Street, London SE17 3LJ, **1094**

Cronin, Léonie, 228 Bellenden Road, London SE15 4BY, **43**

Crook, Paul, 10 St Mary's Crescent, Leamington Spa, Warwickshire CV31 1JL, **410**

Croxford, Mark, 18 Tudor Road, London E9 7SN, **473**

Cruwys, John, Top Flat, 41 Windsor Road, London N7 6JL, **616**

CULLINAN, Edward, CBE RA, Cullinan Studio, 5 Baldwin Terrace, London N1 7RU, **529**, **542**

Cullum, Rosemary, Barn Studio, George Street, Willingham, Cambridge CB24 5LJ, **703**

CUMING, Frederick, RA HON DLitt, The Gables, Iden, Nr Rye, East Sussex TN31 7UY, **29**, **73**, **99**, **203**

CUMMINS, Gus, RA, Harpsichord House, Cobourg Place, Hastings, Sussex TN34 3HY, **168**, **210**, **281**

Cunningham, Holland, 181 East 90th Street, Apartment 28C, New York, NY 10128, United States, **186**

Cutter, Lee, 5 Gooch House, Malthouse Road, London SW11 7AU, **708**

Cutts, Clare, 4 Redland Terrace, Redland, Bristol BS6 6TD, **1248**

D

Dacre, Myles, 10 Brunswick Square, Hove, East Sussex BN3 1EG, **216**

Dalton, Patrick, 2 Spencer Court, Spencer Road, London SW20 0QW, **41**, **1292**

Daly, Ruth, Marysborough House, Glanmire, Cork, Ireland, **352**

Danilenko, Nina, 51 Heathwood Gardens, London SE7 8ES, **256**

DANNATT, Prof. Trevor, OBE RA, 92 Talfourd Road, London SE15 5NZ, **11**, **556**, **557**, **558**, **560**

Dant, Adam, c/o TAG Fine Arts, Unit 129A, Business Design Centre, 52 Upper Street, London N1 0QH, **450**, **1146**

Davenport, Ian, Courtesy of Alan Cristea Gallery, 43 Pall Mall, London SW1Y 5JG, **980**

Davey, Toni, Westmoor, North Hill Road, Minehead, Somerset TA24 5SF, **994**

David, Helen, 1 The Old Hall, South Grove, London N6 6BP, **401**

David Kohn Architects, Bedford House, 125-133 Camden High Street, London NW1 7JR, **591, 606**

Davies, Clancy Gebler, 8 Rossetti Court, Ridgmount Place, London WC1E 7AG, **156, 253**

Davies, Richard, North Space, Salamander Court, 135 York Way, London N7 9LG, **905**

Davis, Stella, 72 Forest Road, Onehouse, Stowmarket, Suffolk IP14 3EP, **810**

de Búrca, Miriam, Courtesy of Alan Cristea Gallery, 43 Pall Mall, London SW1Y 5JG, **990**

DE GREY, Spencer, CBE RA, Foster + Partners, Riverside, Albert Wharf, 22 Hester Road, London SW11 4AN, **645, 664**

de la Cruz, Angela, Courtesy of Lisson Gallery, **747**

de Milo, Varla, 51 Mickleham Road, Orpington, Kent BR5 2RW, **792**

de Monchaux, Cathy, 1 Hoxton Street, London N1 6NL, **857**

de Monchaux, Paul, 56 Manor Avenue, London SE4 1TE, **505**

Deacon, Les, 6 St Jons Close, Higham, Rochester, Kent ME3 7BP, **10**

Deakin, Bob, 3 Stable Cottages, Holmshaw Farm, Layhams Road, Keston, Kent BR2 6AR, **356**

Denton, Mark, c/o Jealous Gallery, 53 Curtain Road, London EC2A 3PT, **402, 435**

Denton, Nigel, 42 Elliott Road, London W4 1PE, **371**

DESMET, Anne, RA, Long & Ryle Contemporary Art, 4 John Islip Street, London SW1P 4PX, **1153**, 22 Queen Anne Road, London E9 7AH, **1151, 1154, 1155, 1156, 1219**

DICKSON, Dr Jennifer, RA, 20 Osborne Street, Ottawa, Ontario K1S 4Z9, Canada **1013, 1014, 1015**

DINE, Jim, HON RA, Courtesy of Alan Cristea Gallery, 43 Pall Mall, London SW1Y 5JG, **1052**

Dixon, Helen, 14 Ellington House, Harper Road, London SE1 6RP, **1235**

Dobson, Roger, 11 Rock Lodge Gardens, Sunderland SR6 9NU, **25**

Dodd, Elliot, 42B Finsen Road, London SE5 9AW, **385**

Dodds, James, c/o Messum's Fine Art, 28 Cork Street, London W1S 3NG, **1035**

Donnelly, Susan, 17 Norlands Lane, Prescot L35 6NR, **1279**

Doubleday, Peter, 9 Chyverton Close, Newquay, Cornwall TR7 2AR, **1224**

Douglas, Emma, 31 Britton Street, London EC1M 5UH, **1217**

DRAPER, Kenneth, RA, Carrer Gran 55A, Es Castell, Menorca, 7720, Spain, **18, 466**

Drury, Dickon, Flat 2, 22 Kellett Road, London SW2 1EB, **55**

DSDHA, 357 Kennington Lane, London SE11 5QY, **648**

Dukes, Robert, 72 Parkside Estate, Rutland Road, London E9 7JY, **453**

Duncan, Sarah, 33 Gwilliam Street, Windmill Hill, Bristol BS3 4LT, **1075**

Dunne, Alan, 8 Gelder Close, Lower Earley, Reading RG6 3US, **294**

DUNSTAN, the late Bernard, RA PPRWA, Courtesy of Chris Beetles Gallery, 8 & 10 Ryder Street, London SW1Y 6QB, **92, 107, 129, 152, 297, 302**

Dury, Sophy, 106 Fitzjohns Avenue, London NW3 6NT, **334**

E

Eason, Greg, 54C Cricketfield Road, London E5 8NS, **899, 900**

Eccles, Hannah, 198 Goldhurst Terrace, London NW6 3HN, **991**

Edmondson, Machiko, Flat 45, Temple House, 5 Fleet Street, Brighton BN1 4HB, **98**

Edwards, Mark, 1 Mansfield Road, Reading RG1 6AL, **13**

Eel, 8 Sudeley Terrace, Brighton BN2 1HD, **215**

Elgersma, Emmely, 25A Stamford Hill, London N16 5TU, **399**

Ellis, Tim, Flat 67, Gladstone House, 31 Dowells Street, London SE10 9FF, **965**

Ellis, Martha, 1-27 Bothwell House, Bothwell Street, Edinburgh EH7 5YL, **1030**

EMIN, Tracey, CBE RA, 1 Tenter Ground, London E1 7NH, **869, 1225, 1226, 1230, 1231**

EPR Architects, 30 Millbank, London SW1P 4DU, **582, 610**

EYTON, Anthony, RA, 166 Brixton Road, London SW9 6AU, **90, 124, 132, 307**

F

Falle, Matt, Matt Falle Art, Caribbean Stores, Dicq Rd, St. Saviour, Jersey, Channel Islands JE2 7PZ, **478**

Farmer, Oscar, 104 Woodhill, London SE18 5JL, **12, 367**

FARTHING, Prof. Stephen, RA, 3 Canterbury Road, Flitwick MK45 1TY, **74, 224, 233, 306**

FaulknerBrowns Architects, Dobson House, Northumbrian Way, Killingworth, Newcastle upon Tyne NE12 6QW, **515, 629**

Fears, Alan, The Spinney, Cliff Hill Lane, Aslockton, Nottingham NG13 9AP, **101**

Ferm, Tom, Flat 2, 26 Mornington Terrace, London NW1 7RS, **589**

Fernandez Saus, Ramiro, c/o Long & Ryle Gallery, 4 John Islip Street, London SW1P 4PX, **343**

Feroda, Pine, Southernhay, North Street, South Molton, Devon EX36 3AN, **1216**

Finlay, Andy, 34 Mountbatten Square, Windsor SL4 1SY, **342**

Fitzmaurice, John, 55 Waldeck Road, London N15 3EL, **383**

Fitzroy, Cornelia, Norton House, Loddon Road, Norton Sub Course, Norwich NR14 6RY, **71**

Fletcher Priest Architects, Middlesex House, 34/42 Cleveland Street, London W1T 4JE, **527, 666**

Flinders, Hannah, 5 Compton Avenue, London N1 2XD, **1289**

Florian Beigel Architects, 17 Tanza Road, London NW3 2UA, **592, 593**

Flory, Peter, 9 Christchurch Gardens, Reading RG2 7AH, **889**

Ford, Laura, 1A Perren Street, London NW5 3ED, **786, 790**

Ford, Peter, 13 Cotswold Road, Windmill Hill, Bristol BS3 4NX, **947**

Ford, Ros, 47 Hill Street, Totterdown, Bristol BS3 4TS, **912**

Forrest-Beckett, Michelle, 43 Washingborough Road, Heighington, Lincoln LN4 1QW, **839**

Forster, Richard, c/o Ingleby Gallery, Edinburgh EH7 5DD, **827**

Forward, Hannah, 12 Scott Road, Hove BN3 5HN, **1184**

FOSTER OF THAMES BANK, Lord, OM RA, Foster + Partners, Riverside, Albert Wharf, 22 Hester Road, London SW11 4AN, **651, 663**

Franks, Stephanie, 7F, 155 Wooster Street, New York, NY 10012, United States, **1233**

Fraser, Beth, 14B Cricketfield Road, London E5 8NS, **53**

FREETH, Peter, RA, 83 Muswell Hill Road, London N10 3HT, **1250, 1251, 1255, 1259, 1260, 1261**

Fretten, Jackie, 23 Malling Street, Lewes, East Sussex BN7 2RA, **159**

Furneaux, Paul, 36/5 Rodney Street, Edinburgh EH7 4DX, **692**

Furstova, Mila, Flat 2, Uplands, Malvern Road, Cheltenham, Gloucestershire GL50 2JH, **1165**

G

Galvin, Sorsha, 17 Garfield Court, London NW6 7SZ, **719**

Game, Julian, 53 Meadway, Ashford TW15 2TJ, **142**

Gander, Ryan, Courtesy of Lisson Gallery, **800**

Gao, Qingsheng, 1706, 117 N 15th Street, Philadelphia, PA 19102, United States, **434**

Gargulinska, Ewa, 1 Gordon Avenue, St Margarets, Twickenham TW1 1NH, **1028**

Gear, Amy, Da Cottage, Freefield, Bridge End, Burra, Shetland ZE2 9LD, **319**

GEDDES, Stewart, HON MEMBER EX OFFICIO PRWA, Royal West of England Academy, 8 Downs Road, Bristol BS9 3TX, **64**

Geden, Dennis, Courtesy of The Redfern Gallery, 20 Cork Street, London W1S 3HL, **214**

Georgi, Hans-Jorg, Everything Ltd, 3 Accurist House, 44 Baker Street, London W1U 7AL, **779**

Gibbs, Stephen, 11 Stanfield Road, Southend-on-Sea, Essex SS2 5DQ, **1126**

Gilbert, Deborah, Flat 2, Hillside Court, Alden Crescent, Headington, Oxford OX3 9NR, **354**

Gill, Jennifer, 109 Calabria Road, London N5 1HS, **961**

Giuseppe Marasco & Mike Quirke, , 54 Basing Hill, London NW11 8TH, **118**

Godfrey, Carl, 17 Sandringham Road, Swindon SN3 1HW, **798**

Goffe, Tim, 30 Ravenswood Road, London SW12 9PJ, **226**

Gomez, Lucia, 334A Perth Road (Pinegrove), Dundee DD2 1EQ, **237**

Gordon, Jackie, 19 Windlesham Gardens, Shoreham-by-sea, West Sussex BN43 5AD, **966**

GORMLEY, Antony, RA, 15-23 Vale Royal, London N7 9AP, **707**, Courtesy of Alan Cristea Gallery, 43 Pall Mall, London SW1Y 5JG, **1238, 1239, 1240**

Gorner, Jo, 1-2 Winters Cottages, Blackshaw Head, Hebden Bridge, West Yorkshire, HX7 7JU, **893, 1269**

Gorner, Veta, Lantern Mill, 10 Church Street, Easton on the Hill, Stamford, Northamptonshire PE9 3LL, **1116**

Gough, Lucy, 43 Mill Road, Lode, Cambridge CB25 9EN, **1148**

Grady, Paul, 107 Princes Road, Middlesbrough TS1 4BN, **471**

Granville, Sarah, 139 Dalling Road, London W6 0ET, **1272**

Gray, Donna, 86 Crown Road, Portslade-by-Sea, Brighton BN41 1SH, **27**

Gray, Helen, 7 Tannery Lane, Guildford GU5 0AD, **694**

Gray, Len, 36 Leyburn Grove, Shipley BD18 3NR, **222**

Grayson, Anna, 57 Yannon Drive, Teignmouth, Devon TQ14 9JP, **288, 300**

GREEN, Anthony, RA, Courtesy of Chris Beetles Gallery, 8 & 10 Ryder Street, London SW1Y 6QB, **4, 7, 16, 1145**

Green, Eleanor, Ground Floor Flat, 38 Credenhill Street, London SW16 6PR, **164**

Green, Nicola, c/o Candida Stevens Gallery, 12 Northgate, Chichester, West Sussex PO19 1BA, **174**

Greenglass, Nick, 126 Cromwell Road, Bristol BS6 5EZ, **1159**

Greenwood, Tom, 38 Gathorne Road, Bristol BS3 1LU, **211**

Greyer, Dominic, 42 Wood Road, Whalley Range, Manchester M16 8BL, **1293**, **1295**

Griffin, Carole, 106 Waxwell Lane, Pinner, Middlesex HA5 3ES, **100**

Griffiths, Anne, 4 Gabriel House, Newbury Street, Wantage OX12 8DJ, **759**

Griffiths, David, 49 Westville Road, Cardiff CF23 5DF, **260**

Grimmer, Martyn, 23 Windsor Terrace, Totterdown, Bristol BS3 4UF, **969**

GRIMSHAW, Sir Nicholas, CBE PPRA, Grimshaw Architects, 57 Clerkenwell Road, London ECIM 5NG, **536**, **537**, **571**, **637**

Groupwork + Amin Taha, 15 Clerkenwell Close, London ECIR OAA, **628**, **650**

Grover, Martin, Flat 2, 31 Morrish Road, London SW2 4EB, **414**

Gudgin, Jemma, 30D Stirling Road, Shortstown, Bedfordshire, MK42 OTY, **470**

Gunn, Susan, Flat 4, Hillfield, Congleton Road, Alderley Edge, Cheshire SK9 7AA, **207**, **481**

Gustafson Porter and Bowman LLP, 1 Cobham Mews, London NW1 9SB, **516**

Gutsche, Claas, Freienwalder Strasse 14, Berlin, 13055, Germany **829**

Guy-Robinson, Graham, The Elms, Georges Lane, Sheviock, Nr Torpoint, Cornwall PLII 3EL, **833**

H

Habisrittinger, Mark, 5 Frankley Buildings, Bath BAI 6EG, **805**

Haines, Beatrice, 26 Bread Street, Warminster, Wiltshire BAI2 8DF, **431**

Hajdamach, Jonathan, 13 Ashley Close, Kingswinford, West Midlands DY6 9SX, **1318**

Hall, Julia, Shoreacre, Vention, Putsborough, Devon EX33 ILD, **1114**

HALL, Nigel, RA, II Kensington Park Gardens, London WII 3HD, **488**, **489**, **842**

Hall, Sharon, 102 Royal Oak Court, Pitfield Street, London NI 6EP, **149**

Hall, Tim, The Net Loft, Eden Place, Mousehole, Penzance, Cornwall, TRI9 6RG, **284**

Halliday, Mark, Cilyrynys, Porthyrhyd, Carmarthenshire SA32 8PX, **739**

Halls, Roxana, 2 Glenhurst Court, Farquhar Road, London SEI9 ISR, **160**

Hamilton, Hector Geoffrey, Flat B, 9 Cambridge Drive, London SEI2 8AG, **1178**

Hammick, Tom, c/o Flowers Gallery, 82 Kingsland Road, London E2 8DP, **1229**

Hammond, Martin, 56 Gypsy Hill, London SE19 1PD, **373**

Hampson, Mark, 16 Dickens Road, Broadstairs, Kent CT10 1DX, **1118**

Hamshaw-Thomas, Hugh, 78 Selwyn Avenue, Highams Park,
London E4 9LR, **1215**

Haptic Architects Ltd, 77 White Lion Street, London N1 9PF, **614**

Haraldsdottir, Bjork, Higher Holditch Farm, Holditch, Chard,
Dorset TA20 4NL, **693**

Hardwick, Bruce, 25 Dublin Road, Intake, Doncaster, South
Yorkshire DN2 5HD, **405**

Hargreaves, Barton, 24 Droridge, Dartington, Totnes, Devon
TQ9 6JQ, **1022**

Harley, Anna, 9 Nutgrove Avenue, Victoria Park, Bristol BS3 4QE,
914

Harnett, Marie, Courtesy of Alan Cristea Gallery, 43 Pall Mall,
London SW1Y 5JG, **1056**

Harper, Andy, Assembly, West Place, St Just TR19 7JB, **95**

Harrington, Siomha, 47 Talfourd Avenue, Reading RG6 7BP, **208**

Harris, Jane, c/o Jill Sheridan, 17 Brodrick Road, London SW17 7DZ,
995

Harris, Sara Jayne, 7 Rodney Road, Walton-on-Thames, Surrey
KT12 3LE, **1047**

Harrison, Matilda, 38 Fortis Green Road, London N10 3HN, **128**

Harrison-Jeive, Bridget, 29 Whitby Road, Milford on Sea,
Lymington, Hampshire SO41 ONE, **65**

Hart, Paul, Walnut House, Somerby Road, Ropsley, Lincolnshire
NG33 4AZ, **1085**

Hatami, Jasmine, 36 Addisland Court, Holland Villas Road,
London W14 8DA, **131**

Hatoum, Mona, **777**

Hauska, Iryna, Kometvagen 53, Stockholm 18348, Sweden **393**

Hawdon, Paul, 9 Worts Causeway, Cambridge CB1 8RJ, **953**

Hawkins Brown, 159 St John Street, London EC1V 4QJ, **652**

Haworth, Emma, 149 Ribblesdale Road, London SW16 6SP, **283**

Haworth Tompkins Architects, Haworth Tompkins Ltd,
33 Greenwood Place, London NW5 1LB, **655, 656**

Hayes, David, 26 Marshcroft Lane, Tring, Hertfordshire HP23 5PP,
238

Hayes Davidson, Studio A, 21 Conduit Place, London W2 1HS, **541**

Hayter, Michael, 32 Repton Road, Brislington, Bristol BS4 3LT, **382**

Head, Oddly, 5 Spruce Hills Road, London E17 4LB, **88, 102**

Heathcote, Maya, 89 Cuckmere Way, Brighton BN1 8GB, **1280**

HEATHERWICK, Thomas, CBE RA, Heatherwick Studio,
356-364 Gray's Inn Road, London WC1X 8BH, **649**

Heaton, Julie, 8 Queensholm Close, Bristol BS16 6LD, **130**

Heeps, Richard, c/o TAG Fine Arts, Unit 129A, Business Design Centre, 52 Upper Street, London N1 0QH, **1092**

Hemsworth, Gerard, Handsel House, Junction Road, Staplecross, Robertsbridge, East Sussex TN32 5SH, **362**

Henry, Ronald, c/o Bethlem Gallery, Bethlem Royal Hospital, Monks Orchard Road, Beckenham, Kent BR3 3BX, **229**

Hensey, Maree, 19 Edenvale Road, Ranelagh, Dublin 6, Ireland, **500**

Herrero, Lorena, Flat 4, 8 Whitmore Road, London N1 5DT, **952**

Hewitson, Dick, Oakley Lodge, 31 Brook Lane, Corfe Mullen, Wimborne, Dorset BH21 3RD, **379**

Heyer, Vera Christine, Schwalbenweg 11, Auenwald 71549, Germany, **398**

Hill, Harry, c/o Independent Talent, 40 Whitfield Street, London W1T 2RH, **370, 395**

Hinchliffe, Peter, 6 Odessa Court, Odessa Road, London E7 9BE, **942**

Hinton, Kevin, Mill Lane House, Mill Lane, Cassington, Witney OX29 4DL, **967**

Hipkiss, Kate, 51 Laburnum Road, Oxford OX2 9EN, **958**

Hipkiss, La Menine, Route D271, Panjas, 32110, France, **1125**

Hirst, Nicky, 12 Grove Park, London SE5 8LR, **493**

HOCKNEY, David, OM CH RA, c/o The Royal Academy of Arts, **879, 880, 1071**

Hodge, Nicky, 53 Evelina Road, London SE15 2DY, **978**

Hodgson, Geoff, Stone Bramble Cottage, Great Comberton, Pershore, Worcestershire WR10 3DP, **1160, 1183**

Hogan, Eileen, 13 Wythburn Place, London W1H 7BU, **333**

Hogarth, Adam, 55 Nutfield Road, London SE22 9DG, **1204**

Hogg, Daniel, 37 Ormonde Road, Wokingham RG41 2RA, **491, 773**

Holmes, Andrew, 27 Leigh Road, London N5 1AH, **690**

Holmes, Michelle, 30 Ashby Road, Newbold, Coleorton, Coalville, Leicestershire LE67 8PB, **232**

Holt, Alison, Highfield, 85 Oakhurst Road, Oswestry, Shropshire SY11 1BL, **293**

Holt, Julie, 416 Worle Moor Road, Weston-super-Mare BS24 7JR, **797**

Holt, Rodney, 47 Poulton Avenue, Lytham St Anne's, Lancashire FY8 3JR, **1286**

Homma, Kaori, 83 Brookbank Road, London SE13 7BZ, **918**

Hooper, Jane, 1 Hill View, Thame Road, Chilton, Aylesbury HP18 9LL, **269**

HOPKINS, Sir Michael, CBE RA, Hopkins Architects Partnership LLP, 27 Broadley Terrace, London NW1 6LG, **533, 534**

Horovitz, Michael, OBE, MH New Departures-Poetry Olympics, PO Box 9819, London W11 2GQ, **377**

Hosking, Paul, Flat 1, 1 Teesdale Street, London E2 6GF, **813, 814**

Hoskins, Stephen, 3 Sandcroft Avenue, Uphill, Weston-super-Mare BS23 4SS, **982**

HOWARD, Ken, OBE RA, 8 South Bolton Gardens, London SW5 0DH, **50, 165, 236, 273**

Howell, Morgan, 4 Prae Close, St Albans AL3 4SF, **485**

Howie, Sonya, 11 Saffron House, 5 Ramsgate Street, London E8 2FH, **36**

HTA Design LLP, 78 Chamber Street, London E1 8BL, **604**

Hubbard, Steven, 1 Berkeley Villas, Lower Street, Stroud, Gloucestershire GL5 2HU, **1023**

Hudson, Laura, 205 Cardamom Building, 31 Shad Thames, London SE1 2YR, **380**

Hugh Strange Architects, 210 Evelyn Street, London SE8 5BZ, **579**

Huglin, David, Flat 1, 60 Sunningfields Road, London NW4 4RL, **1142**

HUME, Gary, RA, Courtesy of Blackbird Pictures Ltd, 54 - 56 Peartree Street, London EC1V 3SV, **135, 324**

Humphreys, John, Beach Crest, Normans Bay, East Sussex BN24 6PS, **507**

Hurdwell, James, The Flat, 153A Corve Street, Ludlow, Shropshire SY8 2PG, **828**

Huri, Ione, Rutland Gate 62/10, London SW7 1PJ, **245**

Hurman, Sue, 3 Mountfields, Brighton BN1 7BT, **1329**

Hutcheon, Lawrie, 52B Larkhall Rise, London SW4 6JY, **496, 1174**

HUTTON, Louisa OBE RA and Matthias Sauerbruch, 74 Ledbury Road, London W11 2AH, **623, 682**

HUXLEY, Prof. Paul, RA, 2 Dalling Road, London W6 0JB, **69, 234, 1187**

HYMAN, Timothy, RA, 62 Myddelton Square, London EC1R 1XX, **31, 45, 876, 1181**

I

Illari, Dario, c/o Jealous Gallery, 53 Curtain Road, London EC2A 3PT, **84**

Ingman, Steven, 157 Markeaton Street, Derby DE22 3AW, **308**

Ingram, Peter, 18A Union Street, Pocklington, East Riding YO42 2JN, **193**

J

JACKLIN, Bill, RA, Courtesy of Marlborough Fine Art,
6 Albemarle Street, London W1S 4BY, **76, 854, 856, 1025, 1170, 1179**

Jackson, Alison, 134 Lots Road, London SW10 0RJ, **163**

JACKSON, Vanessa, RA, 169 Bermondsey Street, London SE1 3UW, **56, 296, 853, 871**

Jacobsen, Inge, 20 Haldane Place, London SW18 4UH, **201**

James, C., 152 Portway, London E15 3QW, **350**

James, Juliet, 22 Ilex Green, Hailsham, East Sussex BN27 1TR, **154, 251**

Jamieson, Laura, 7 Queens Walk, Cleveleys, Lancashire FY5 1JU, **223**

Jansson, Linda Sofie, 15 Hunting Close, Keam House, Esher, Surrey KT10 8PB, **228**

JARAY, Tess, RA, Lion East Apartment, 24 North Road, London N7 9EA, **217**, Courtesy of Nutmeg Editions, 81 Southey Road, London N15 5LJ, **1054**

Jean, Evelyn, Flat 4, 5A Craven Road, London W2 3BP, **290**

JEFFRIES, Neil, RA, 40 Allfarthing Lane, London SW18 2AJ, **8, 741, 848, 849, 963, 964**

Jestico + Whiles, Sutton Yard, 65 Goswell Road, London EC1V 7EN, **599, 600**

Jewitt-Harris, Jennie, 36 Upper Park Road, Camberley, Surrey GU15 2EF, **461, 464**

JIRICNA, Eva, CBE RA, 10B Randolph Crescent, London W9 1DR, **538, 539**

JOFFE, Prof. Chantal, RA, Courtesy of the artist and Victoria Miro, London / Venice, **304**

John McAslan + Partners, 7-9 William Road, London NW1 3ER, **583**

Johnson, Ben, 4 St Peters Wharf, Chiswick Mall, London W6 9UD, **323**

Johnson, Holli Mae, 475 The Heart, Walton-on-Thames, Surrey KT12 1GE, **287**

Johnson Soliz, Cecile, 166 Kings Road, Cardiff CF11 9DG, **726**

Johnson, Steve, 33 Pond Road, London SE3 0SE, **687**

Johnson, Wilma, 6 Redston Road, London N8 7HJ, **117**

JONES, Allen, RA, 41 Charterhouse Square, London EC1M 6EA, **742, 883, 1264**

Jones, Edward, 43A Richmond Road, Montpelier, Bristol BS6 5EN, **760**

Jones, Hannah, Flat 36, 22 Tidemill Way, London SE8 4BF, **1180**

Jones, Katherine, Flat 5, Greenleaf Close, London SW2 2HB, **959, 1152**

Jones, Lucy, c/o Flowers Gallery, 82 Kingsland Road, London E2 8DP, **463**

Jones, Peter, 25 North Street, St Leonards-on-Sea, East Sussex TN38 0EX, **407, 424**

Josef, Billie, Flat 2, 19 Ridge Road, London N8 9LE, **1117**

Joshua Cooper, Thomas, c/o Ingleby Gallery, 6 Carlton Terrace, Edinburgh EH7 5DD, **826**

Joyce, James, 10 Blossom Street, London E1 6PL, **492**

JULIEN, Isaac, CBE RA, Courtesy of the artist and Victoria Miro, London N1 5PW, **220, 688, 922**

Jury Morgan, Toby, Unit 3, 718-722 Seven Sisters Road, London N15 5NH, **1189**

K

KAPOOR, Sir Anish, CBE RA, **1**

Karayaka, Lale, Otto Malling Gade 6, 4th, Copenhagen 2100, Denmark, **116**

Karim, Farid, 78 Daryngton Drive, London UB6 8BL, **601**

Kays, Hayden, c/o Jealous Gallery, 53 Curtain Road, London EC2A 3PT, **44, 1194**

Keith Williams Architects, 74 Long Lane, London SE1 4AU, **574, 643**

Kellett, Oli, 37 Lower Park Road, Hastings TN34 2LA, **480, 683**

Kelly, Bryan, 21 Southam Road, Dunchurch, Rugby CV22 6NL, **68**

Kennedy, Michael, 107 Knights Croft, New Ash Green, Longfield, Kent DA3 8HY, **277**

Kerkar, Subodh, Museum of Goa, Plot No. 79, Pilerne Industrial Estate, Pilerne, Bardez, Goa 403511, India, **1200**

Kevans, Annie, Lieu Dit 'La Bole Noire', Proissans 24200, France **1291**

Khan, Idris, Courtesy of the artist and Victoria Miro, London / Venice, **198**

KIEFER, Anselm, HON RA, Courtesy of the artist and White Cube Ltd, 144-152 Bermondsey Street, London SE1 3TQ, **861**

Kim, c/o Bethlem Gallery, Bethlem Royal Hospital, Monks Orchard Road, Beckenham, Kent BR3 3BX, **39**

King, Leonie, Oranmore Castle, Galway, Ireland, **1123**

KING, Prof. Phillip, CBE PPRA, Courtesy of Thomas Dane Gallery, 11 Duke Street, London SW1Y 6BN, **1347**

Kirkbride, Michael, 33 Barnwood Road, Earby, Lancashire BB18 6PB, **191**

Kirwan, Richard, 72 Sandmere Road, London SW4 7QH, **1206**

Kitchen, Jo, 219A Gladstone Avenue, London N22 6LB, **394**

Kitching, Alan, Courtesy of Advanced Graphics London, 68 Walcot Square, London SE11 4TZ, **1273**

KNEALE, Prof. Bryan, RA, Courtesy of Pangolin London, Kings Place, 90 York Way, London N1 9AG, **48, 712, 715, 716, 836, 837**

Knight, Sophie Lourdes, 22548 Ravensbury Avenue, Los Altos Hills, CA 94024-6432, United States, **261**

Knox Bhavan Architects LLP, 69 Choumert Road, London SE15 4AR, **617**

Ko, Anthony Chun Ming, Flat A, 7/F, Block 9, City Garden, Wharf Street, North Point, Hong Kong, **1077**

Ko, Dong-Hwan, 44 Malden Court, West Barnes Lane, New Malden KT3 4PP, **811**

Kohn Pedersen Fox, 7A Langley Street, London WC2H 9JA, **670, 675**

Kolker, Richard, 30 Carlos Street, Godalming, Surrey GU7 1BP, **179**

KORALEK, Paul, CBE RA, 3 Rochester Road, London NW1 9JH, **563, 564, 565, 566**

Kravchenko, Aleksandra, 17B Caversham Road, London NW5 2DT, **639**

L

Lambert, Alison, Studio 6, Canal Warehouse, Leicester Row, Coventry, West Midlands, CV1 4LH, **1133, 1139**

Lambert, Terence, 72 Keldregate, Huddersfield HD2 1TB, **151, 744**

LANDY, Michael, RA, Courtesy of Thomas Dane Gallery, 3 Duke Street, London SW1Y 6BN, **483, 1344**

Lang, Liane, 6 Northleigh House, Powis Road, London E3 3NL, **1104**

Langford, Martin, 59 Crest Gardens, Ruislip HA4 9HB, **1143**

Langgaard, Louise, Soender Boulevard 58, 2 tv, Copenhagen V, 1720, Denmark **37**

Langlands & Bell, Courtesy of Alan Cristea Gallery, 43 Pall Mall, London SW1Y 5JG, **1149**

Latto, Kay, Belvedere Villa, 35 Palace Road, Ripon, North Yorkshire, HG4 1EZ, **1340**

Lavelle, Bryan, 24 Acremen Street, Cerne Abbas, Dorchester, Dorset DT2 7JX, **390**

Lawler, John, 145 Beaver Trail, Hattiesburg, MS 39401, United States, **1144**

Lawrence, Philippa, Studio 21, Spike Island, 133 Cumberland Road, Bristol BS1 6UX, **968, 981**

Lawrenson, Emma, Ivy Bank Farmhouse, Sheffield Road, Jackson Bridge, Holmfirth HD9 7HB, **1210, 1211**

Lawson, Debbie, 185A Stoke Newington Church Street, London N16 0UL, **436**

Lawson, Simon, 20 Allfarthing Lane, London SW18 2PQ, **1262**

LAWSON, Sonia, RA, 39 Stoke Road, Linslade, Leighton Buzzard LU7 2SW, **161**

Lazerwitz, Emily, 7A Heath Street, London NW3 6TP, **752**

LE BRUN, Christopher, PRA, c/o the Royal Academy, **1244**, **1245**, **1246**, **1247**, **1352**

Leach, Ursula, Old Forge Cottage, Iwerne Minster, Dorset DT11 8LX, **1039**

Lee, Andrew, 34 Prospect House, Donegal Street, London N1 9QD, **1278**

Lee, Guisun, Flat 77, Invicta, Millennium Promenade, Bristol BS1 5SX, **206**

Lee, Sara, 6 Westcombe Park Road, London SE3 7RB, **1012**, **1027**

Lehrer, Avi, 11 Rechov Hamatzor, Jerusalem 9254464, Israel, **24**

Leigh, Dene, 557 Eastern Avenue, Ilford, Essex IG2 6PJ, **972**

Leighton, Donna, Flat 5, 17 Cromwell Road, London SW7 2JB, **954**, **956**

Lewis, Alexander, 82 Billet Road, London E17 5DN, **720**, **830**

Lewis, Cathy, Studio 44, Spike Island, 133 Cumberland Road, Bristol BS1 6UX, **447**, **460**

Lewis, Stephen, Harold Works, 6 Creekside, London SE8 4SA, **697**

Lewis, Tim, c/o Flowers Gallery, 82 Kingsland Road, London E2 8DP, **1265**

Lifschutz Davidson Sandilands, Island Studios, 22 St Peter's Square, London W6 9NW, **572**, **669**

Lim, C. J., 95 Greencroft Gardens, London NW6 3PG, **544**, **551**

Lloyd, Jonathan, 18 Ramseys Lane, Wooler, Northumberland NE71 6NR, **1138**

Loffill, Tom, 280 Queen's Road, London SE14 5JN, **1095**

Löhr, Alf, 3 East View, Vale of Health, London NW3 1AU, **807**

Lomaka, Olga, Flat A, 131 Beaufort Street, London SW3 6BS, **265**

Lomax, Tom, 6 Friendly Street, London SE8 4DT, **1191**

Long, Fiona, Cubitt Artists, 8 Angel Mews, London N1 9HH, **150**

LONG, Sir Richard, CBE RA, Courtesy of Alan Cristea Gallery, 43 Pall Mall, London SW1Y 5JG, **948**, Courtesy of Lisson Gallery, **1348**

Love, Johanna, 285B Underhill Road, London SE22 0AN, **983**

Lovell, Andy, Ashleigh, Gloucester Street, Painswick, Gloucestershire GL6 6QN, **1084**

Lovett, Caroline, 161 Rushmere Road, Ipswich, Suffolk IP4 3LB, **113**

Lowe, Oscar, 30-32 Havelock Walk, London SE23 3HG, **1109**

Lowers, Michael, 12 Creasy Estate, Aberdour Street, London SE1 4SL, **403**, **404**

Lycett, Joe, 320 Greenhouse, Custard Factory, Birmingham B9 4DP, **396**

Macfarlane, Barbara, 2A Conway Street, Fitzroy Square, London WIT 6BA, **158**

MACH, Prof. David, RA, 8 Havelock Walk, London SE23 3HG, **437, 455, 459, 504, 695**

Mach, Robert, 32 Crescent Road, Lundin Links, Leven, Fife KY8 6AE, **408**

Mackechnie, John, 6 Holyrood Crescent, Glasgow G20 6HJ, **1199**

Madeley, Chris, 89 Rowditch Furlong, Milton Keynes MK14 5FD, **501**

Magill, Anne, 189 Cooden Drive, Bexhill-on-Sea, East Sussex TN39 3AQ, **898**

MAINE, John, RA, The Old School, East Knoyle, Salisbury, Wiltshire SP3 6AF, **42, 835, 1349, 1350**

Maiofis, Gregori, c/o Marina Shtager, Studio 24, 87 Crampton Street, London SE17 3AZ, **1236, 1237**

Mallo Ferrer, Diego, Rambla del Poblenou 44, 4, 1, Barcelona, 8005, Spain, **1057**

Mannan, Haider, Mannan LTD, 71-75 Shelton Street, London WC2H 9JQ, **338**

Maple, Sarah, 9 Heron Close, Langley Green, Crawley, West Sussex RH11 7QX, **200**, c/o Jealous Gallery, 53 Curtain Road, London EC2A 3PT, **1294**

Mara, Alice, 6 Market Street, Lewes, East Sussex BN7 2NB, **1192**

Marks Barfield Architects, 50 Bromells Road, London SW4 0BG, **654**

Marsden, William, Flat GH, Enterprize House, 2 Tudor Grove, London E9 7QL, **325**

Martin, Garry, 44 Lingfield Road, Edenbridge TN8 5DX, **1343**

Martin, Marie-Louise, 14 Elston Place, Aldershot, Hampshire GU12 4HY, **1188**

Martin, Paul, Brooke House, Nyewood, Petersfield, Hampshire GU31 5JA, **1076**

Martin, Ruth, Studio 311, Cockpit Arts, 18-22 Creekside, London SE8 3DZ, **1190, 1193**

Martin, Sonia, 63B Kennington Park Road, London SE11 4JQ, **1134**

Matthews, Peter, 44 Astley Way, Ashby, Leicestershire LE65 1LY, **1000**

Mauro, Matteo, Flat 1, 139 Walm Lane, London NW2 3AU, **594**

Mazzolari, Carolina, 2 Millfields Road, Clapton Pond, London E5 0SB, **803**

MccGwire, Kate, Unit 501A, Platts Eyot Island, Lower Sunbury Road, Hampton TW12 2HF, **881**

McClure, Calum, 372, 2/1 Langside Road, Glasgow G42 8XR, **951**

McCOMB, Dr Leonard, RA, c/o Royal Academy of Arts, London **26**, **40**, **47**, **877**

McCrae, Chris, Longbury, Rock Road, Storrington, West Sussex RH20 3AH, **406**

McDaid, Carol, 53 Farrant Avenue, London N22 6PD, **975**

McDougall, Thomas, Flat 30, Bath House, 25 Dunbridge Street, London E2 6JD, **178**

McFADYEN, Jock, RA, c/o Royal Academy of Arts, London, **360**, **482**, **902**, **1053**

McKEEVER, Prof. Ian, RA, Courtesy of Alan Cristea Gallery, 43 Pall Mall, London SW1Y 5JG, **204**, Cowgrove Farm, Hartgrove, Shaftesbury, Dorset, SP7 0AT, **804**, **1197**, **1198**

McKenzie, Jordan, 15 Thomas Hollywood House, Approach Road, London E2 9NB, **205**

McKENZIE SMITH, Dr Ian, CBE HON MEMBER EX OFFICIO PPRSA, Heron House, Montrose, Angus DD10 9TJ, **941**

McLaughlin, Ben, 33 Liddell Gardens, London NW10 3QA, **192**, **1043**

McManners, Jill, Bradfield Hall, Tutts Clump, Bradfield, Reading RG7 6LJ, **438**

McMillan, Jeff, **753**, **765**

McMullan, Kirsty, Flat 6, 126 Highbury New Park, London N5 2DR, **532**

McMurray, Grace, 31 Ardenlee Crescent, Belfast BT6 8QN, **347**

McNicoll, Carol, 3 Charlton Kings Road, London NW5 2SB, **1327**

Melvin, Johanna, 20 St Barnabas Road, London E17 8JY, **381**

Melvin, Rod, 20 St Barnabas Road, London E17 8JY, **110**, **1283**

Merchant, Chitra, 28 Laurel Street, Kingswood, Bristol BS15 8NB, **1120**

Merrick, Nicholas, 18 Michael Crescent, Horley, Surrey RH6 7LH, **140**

Metropolitan Workshop LLP, 14-16 Cowcross Street, London EC1M 6DG, **524**, **586**

Mifsud, Matthew, Flat 59, Effra Court, Brixton Hill, London SW2 1RB, **262**

Mikhail Riches, 15-29 Windsor Street, London N1 8QG, **630**

Miller, Gary, 5 Whyterose Terrace, Aberhil, Leven, Fife KY8 3AP, **419**

Miller, Graeme, Toynbee Studios, 28 Commercial Street, London E1 6AB, **783**

Milner, Janet, 52 Dyne Road, London NW6 7DS, **927**

MILROY, Lisa, RA, Flat 1, Hega House, Ullin Street, London
EI4 6PN, **320, 700, 704**

Minas, Michael, Adelaide Cottage, 51 Park Road, Teddington
TWII OAU, **462**

MISTRY, Prof. Dhruva, CBE RA, 16 Kasturba Nagar, Rt. Bh/d
Ayappa Temple & Nutan School, New Sama Road, Sama
Vadodara, Gujarat, 390024, India, **775**

Mitsola, Sofia, Flat 78, 49 Hallam Street, London WIW 6JP, **409**

Molineaux Boon, Jane, 8 Sloane Gardens, Orpington, Kent
BR6 8PG, **153**

Moore, Gregory, Flat 3/1, 9 Craigmillar Road, Glasgow G42 9JZ, **903**

Moors, Georgia, 133F Chatham Street, London SEI7 IPA, **486**

Moradkhani, Azita, c/o The Cynthia Corbett Gallery, 15 Claremont
Lodge, 15 The Downs, London SW20 8UA, **415, 416**

Morey de Morand, C., 61D Oxford Gardens, London WIO 5UJ, **387**

Morgan, Jane, 45 Bridewell Place, Brewhouse Lane, London
EIW 2PB, **1332**

Morling, Katharine, Cockpit Arts, Studio 205, 18-22 Creekside,
London SE8 3DZ, **782**

Morris, Aimee, Halleys Yard, Earnbank Road, Crieff, Perthshire,
PH7 3HL, **1337**

Morris, Guy, 15 Brewhouse Lane, Rowsham, Buckinghamshire,
HP22 4QT, **1326**

Morris, Jackie H., Aurora, 79 Etnam Street, Leominster,
Herefordshire, HR6 8AE, **840**

MORRIS, Mali, RA, APT Studios Harold Wharf, 6 Creekside,
London SE8 4SA, **298, 475, 476, 1161**

Mortimer, James, Top Floor, 24 The Circus, Bath BAI 2EU, **1277**

MOUSSAVI, Prof. Farshid, RA, Farshid Moussavi Architecture,
12F Floor, 130 Fenchurch Street, London EC3M 5DJ, **642**

Moxhay, Suzanne, Flat 2, Edgehill Lodge, 153 Turnham Road,
London SE4 2LY, **727**

Muir, Sally, 11 Southstoke Road, Combe Down, Bath BA2 5SJ, **444**

Muller, Sigrid, Ty Dulais, Bethlehem, Llandeilo, Carmarthenshire
SAI9 6YH, **710**

Murphy, Anthony, 11 Deckham Terrace, Gateshead NE8 3UY, **771**

N

Nakajima, Fumiko, Cyuo-cho, 5-2-47, Higashikurume-shi, Tokyo
2030054, Japan, **1032**

Narita, Miyako, 18B Ashby Street, London ECIV OED, **331**

NASH, David, OBE RA, Capel Rhiw, Blaenau Ffestiniog, Gwynedd,
North Wales LL41 3NT, **711, 732**

NAUMAN, Bruce, HON RA, c/o Sperone Westwater, 257 Bowery, New York, NY 10002, United States, **802**

Neave, Gloria, Langley Bottom Farm, Hitchin SG4 7PJ, **89**

NELSON, Mike, RA, 7 Peckarmans Wood, London SE26 6RY, **2**

Nelson, Rod, Old Lealand Cottage, Box, Stroud, Gloucestershire, GL6 9HL, **1220**

Neudecker, Mariele, 26 Hengrove Road, Knowle, Bristol BS4 2PS, **984, 1101**

Nevay, Heather, Flat 4, 15 Princes Gardens, Hyndland, Glasgow GI2 9HR, **80**

Newcombe, Rika, 94 Ainsworth Street, Cambridge CB1 2PD, **1232**

Newell Price, Peter, 82 Upland Road, London SE22 0DE, **490**

Newens, David, 8 Kindleton, Great Linford, Milton Keynes MK14 5EA, **270**

Newhall, Justin, Flat C, 37 Belsize Park Gardens, London NW3 4JJ, **321, 1093**

Nex—Architecture, 6-9 Charterhouse Square, London ECIM 6EY, **619**

Ng, Jerome, Flat 11, 36 Churchway, London NWI 2AT, **514**

Níall McLaughlin Architects, Bedford House, 125-133 Camden High Street, London NWI 7JR, **641**

Nicholas Hare Architects, 3 Barnsbury Square, London NI IJL, **611**

Niman, Richard, 6 Camden Studios, 28 Camden Street, London NWI 0LG, **428**

Noble, Paul, Courtesy of Alan Cristea Gallery, 43 Pall Mall, London SWIY 5JG, **1162, 1164**

Noonan, Mo, Mill Hill, Grange Road, Tiptree, Essex CO5 0UL, **348**

O

O'Brien, Emer, Emer O'Brien Studio, Unit 6c, Europa Trading Estate, Fraser Road, Erith, Kent DA8 IQL, **1195**

OCEAN, Prof. Humphrey, RA, 22 Marmora Road, London SE22 0RX, **326, 332, 474**

Ockenden, Louise, 10 Batson Street, London WI2 9PQ, **944, 945**

O'Connell, Angela, 58A Cranley Gardens, London NI3 4LS, **96**

O'DEA, Mick, HON MEMBER EX OFFICIO PRHA, Royal Hibernian Academy of Arts, 15 Ely Place, Dublin D02 A213, Ireland, **180**

O'Donnell, Blake, East Haxted, Haxted Road, Edenbridge, Kent TN8 6PT, **1319**

O'DONOGHUE, Hughie, RA, Courtesy of Marlborough Fine Art, 6 Albemarle Street, London WI5 4BY, **3, 724**

O'Keefe, Kevin, 40 Osborne Road, Southville, Bristol BS3 IPW, **1212**

Okun, Sasha, The Orchard, California Lane, Bushey, Hertfordshire WD23 IES, **859**

Olchowska, Malgorzata, Justitiestraat 4, Antwerp 2018, Belgium, **1271**

O'Leary, Sophie, 8 Mulready House, Marsham Street, London SW1P 4JL, **86**

Oliver, Marilene, Beaux Arts, 48 Maddox Street, London W1S 1AY, **937**

O'Mahony, Michael, 77 Old Park Road, London N13 4RG, **1254**

O'Mara, Lesley, 102 College Road, London SE21 7HW, **167**

O'Mara, Lucienne, 27 Waveney Avenue, London SE15 3UF, **384**

O'Neill, Nigel, 20 Chancery House, Lowood Street, London E1 0BU, **327, 328**

Opie, Julian, Courtesy of Alan Cristea Gallery, 43 Pall Mall, London SW1Y 5JG, **1268**

Orms, 1 Oliver's Yard, 55-71 City Road, London EC1Y 1HQ, **658**

ORR, Prof. Chris, MBE RA, 5 Anhalt Road, London SW11 4NZ, **925, 926, 928, 929, 930**

Overill, Ralph, 10 Foxleigh, Billericay, Essex CM12 9NS, **1218**

P

PALADINO, Mimmo, HON RA, Artist's Collection, 82020, Italy, **864**

Palchaudhuri, Paramita, 32 Campbell Court, 3 Embry Road, London SE9 6BT, **353**

Panchal, Shanti, 11A Graham Road, Harrow HA3 5RP, **190**

Papanastasiu, Andreas, Flat 15, Thompson House, 200 Wornington Road, London W10 5RE, **822, 1049**

PARKER, Cornelia, OBE RA, Courtesy of Alan Cristea Gallery, 43 Pall Mall, London SW1Y 5JG, **1060, 1061, 1062, 1069**, Courtesy of Frith Street Gallery, **1202**

Parker, Helen, Beechwood End, Beechwood Road, Combe Down, Bath BA2 5JU, **989**

Parkhouse, Samantha, 20 Compton Way, Farnham GU10 1QZ, **863**

Parks, Bob, Everything Ltd, 3 Accurist House, 44 Baker Street, London W1U 7AL, **291**

Parnell Eve, Imoca Studios, Schoolhouse Lane, Dublin 8, Ireland, **1034**

Parr, Martin, **1320, 1321, 1322, 1323, 1324, 1325**

PARRY, Eric, RA, Eric Parry Architects, 28-42 Banner Street, London EC1Y 8QE, **587**

Parsons, Stella, The White Cottage, Hawkenbury Road, Tonbridge, Kent TN12 0DU, **241**

Parsons, Vicken, Courtesy of Alan Cristea Gallery, 43 Pall Mall, London SW1Y 5JG, **767, 768**

Parusel, Brigitte, 65A Jerningham Road, London SE14 5NH, **943, 1026**

Patel Taylor, 48 Rawstorne Street, London EC1V 7ND, **522, 528**

Payne, Freya, c/o Flowers Gallery, 82 Kingsland Road, London E2 8DP, **1066, 1067**

Payne, Mandy, 24 Moorside, Lodge Moor, Sheffield S10 4LN, **1252**

Peacock, Elva, 27 The Cedars, Fleet, Hampshire GU51 3YL, **146**

Peake, Fabian, 1 Woodstock Road, London N4 3ET, **316, 389**

Peall, Nicholas, 173A Camberwell New Road, London SE5 0TJ, **254**

Pearman, Edd, 24 Green Lane, London W7 2PB, **1074**

Peintner, Julia, 78 Hilborough Court, Livermere Road, London E8 4LQ, **1063**

Pellegrino, Rossanne, 66 Churchview Road, Twickenham TW2 5BU, **819**

Pello, Freedom Creations, Third Floor, 86-90 Paul Street, London EC2A 4NE, **1185**

Penoyre & Prasad, c/o Sarah Drake, 28-42 Banner Street, London EC1Y 8QE, **590**

Pentlow, Clare, 5 Sidney Road, Rugby CV22 5LA, **946**

PERRY, Grayson, CBE RA, Courtesy of the artist and Victoria Miro, London / Venice, **776**, Courtesy of the artist and Paragon | Contemporary Editions Ltd., **908**

Perry, Mike, Ffynnonofi, Dinas Cross, Newport, Pembrokeshire, SA42 0SD, **743**

Peter Barber Architects, c/o Peter Barber, 173 King's Cross Road, London WC1X 9BZ, **511, 647**

PHILLIPS, Tom, CBE RA, 57 Talfourd Road, London SE15 5NN, **54, 105, 1004, 1005, 1006, 1007**

Phillips, Tooney, Mews House, 84 Becklow Road, London W12 9HJ, **1110**

Philpott, Simon, 31A Cranfield Road, London SE4 1TN, **137**

PIANO, Senator Renzo, HON RA, Renzo Piano Building Workshop, Via P. Paolo Rubens 29 - 16158, Genova, Italy, **562**

Piercy, Sioban, Rahard, Athenry, Galway H65 CD51, Ireland, **1196**

Piercy & Company, The Centro Building, 39 Plender Street, London NW1 0DT, **585**

PILKINGTON, Prof. Cathie, RA, 16 Steeple Court, Coventry Road, London E1 5QZ, **503, 1106, 1107, 1112, 1113, 1115**

Pincis, Kasper, Flat 9, Sassoon House, St Mary's Road, London SE15 2EF, **341, 1108**

Pitts, Joy, Clayworth Cottage, Little Hallam Hill, Ilkeston, Derbyshire DE7 4LY, **1282, 1290**

PLP Architecture, c/o Neil Merryweather, PLP Architecture, 2 Seething Lane, London EC3N 4AT, **671, 676**

Poliak, Diana, The Riding Light, Gravesend Road, Wrotham, Sevenoaks, Kent TN15 7JJ, **1287**

Pollard, Nik, 51 Concorde Drive, Bristol BS10 6PY, **1186**

Populous, 14 Blades Court, London SW15 2NU, **640**

Portus, Rosamund, 5 Prospect Place, Cirencester, Gloucestershire, GL7 1EZ, **374**

Power, Elizabeth, 20 Dynham Road, London NW6 2NR, **372**

Prada, Ana, 8 Manor Way, London SE3 9EF, **801**

Prendergast, Kathy, **757, 758**

Price, Debbie, 7 Clarence Road, Teddington TW11 0BQ, **1044**

Price, Trevor, 23 Blue Anchor Lane, London SE16 3UL, **1140**

Prosek, James, 65 Kachele Street, Easton, CT 6612, United States **145**

Ptolemy Dean Architects Ltd, Calvert's Buildings, 52B Borough High Street, London SE1 1XN, **632**

Publica, 10 Clerkenwell Green, London EC1R 0DP, **512**

Q Queen Sonja of Norway, Her Majesty, **1080**

R R, Tal, Courtesy of the artist and Victoria Miro, London / Venice, **867**

Rackowe, Nathaniel, **815**

RAE, Dr Barbara, CBE RA, c/o Royal Academy of Arts, London **279, 312, 1072, 1078, 1079**

RAE, Fiona, RA, c/o Royal Academy of Arts, London **57, 81, 252, 299**

Ramage, Nik, Old Trecastle Farm, Pen-y-clawdd, Monmouth NP25 4BW, **1346**

RANDALL-PAGE, Peter, RA, Veet Mill Farm, Crockernwell, Devon EX6 6NL, **884, 885, 1087**

Raven, Rosie, 2c Park Road, London E15 3QP, **1331**

Ravenscroft, Ben, 101 Manwood Road, London SE4 1SA, **336, 359**

Reed, Rob, 2 Fordham Close, Hornchurch RM11 3AE, **67**

Reeves, Vic, Bay Tree House, 31 Dymchurch Road, Hythe, Kent CT21 6JE, **772**

Reford, Kitty, 21 Lushington Road, Manningtree, Essex CO11 1EE, **987, 988**

REGO, Dame Paula, DBE RA, Courtesy of Marlborough Fine Art, 6 Albemarle Street, London W1S 4BY, **1208**

Reisner, Yael, 54 Compayne Gardens, London NW6 3RY, **552, 554**

Relly, Tamsin, Flat 4, Stambourne House, Lansdowne Way, London SW8 2DH, **955**

REMFRY, David, MBE RA, 19 Palace Gate, London W8 5LS, **62, 78, 317, 865**

Renneisen, Max, The Weald, Pebblehill Road, Betchworth, RH3 7BP, **23**

Richardson, Simon, Flat 7, 30 Streatham Place, London SW2 4QY, **249**

Rigg, Lisa, 59 Cleveleys Road, London E5 9JW, **30**

Riitta Ikonen, Karoline Hjorth &, Siebkes Gate 4C, Oslo 562, Norway, **111**

Riley, Simone, 1B Wallands Crescent, Lewes, East Sussex BN7 2QT, **1131**

Riman, Jacob, Flat 141, Floor 14, Rivermill One, Lewisham Gateway, London SE13 5FS, **672**

RITCHIE, Prof. Ian, CBE RA, Ian Ritchie Architects, 110 Three Colt Street, London E14 8AZ, **580, 906, 907, 909, 910**

Rivans, Maria, Coronation Studios, 104 North Road, Brighton, East Sussex BN1 1YE, **1122**

Roberts, Jennifer, 5A Cambridge Road, Hove BN3 1DE, **689**

Roberts, Michael, 44 Effra Parade, London SW2 1PZ, **301**

Robeson, Fred, c/o Jeroen van Dooren, 1 Rymer Road, Croydon, Surrey CR0 6EF, **1147**

Robin, Wendy, Elford Mews, 93 Hambalt Road, London SW4 9EQ, **1209**

Robles Hidalgo, Bernardo, Flat 4, 3 Carlisle Lane, London SE1 7LH, **243**

Rodway, Beth, 70 Northwold Road, London E5 8RL, **469**

Rogers, Sarah, Knockarigg Cottage, Knockarigg, Grangecon, County Wicklow W91 W6K2, Ireland, **1128**

ROGERS OF RIVERSIDE, Lord, CH RA, Rogers Stirk Harbour + Partners, The Leadenhall Building, 122 Leadenhall Street, London EC3V 4AB, **624, 626, 631, 644**

Rollason, Jane, Coles Farm, Coles Lane, South Petherton, Somerset TA13 5AF, **1137**

ROONEY, Mick, RA, Courtesy of The Fosse Gallery, The Manor House, The Square, Stow-on-the-Wold, Gloucestershire, GL54 1AF, **35, 83, 240, 275, 289**, 1 Sandford Rise, Charlbury, Chipping Norton, Oxfordshire OX7 3SZ, **1163**

Rothenstein, Anne, 93 Talbot Road, London W2 5JW, **85, 119**

ROTHSCHILD, Eva, RA, Unit 43A, Regents Studios, 8 Andrews Road, London E8 4QN, **737**

Rouncefield, Cecilia, 1 Dowry Square, Bristol BS8 4SH, **933**

Roy, c/o Bethlem Gallery, Bethlem Royal Hospital, Monks Orchard Road, Beckenham, Kent BR3 3BX, **15**

Rudman, Michael, 49 Wood Lane, London N6 5UD, **1267**

Rudziak, Karl, 18 Pembroke Road, Old Portsmouth PO1 2NR, **196**

RUSCHA, Ed, HON RA, Courtesy the artist, Gagosian Gallery, WC1X 9JD, **769**

Russon, Bobbie, 111 Stillingfleet Road, Barnes, London SW13 9AF, **454**

Ryan, Ian, 60 The Chase, Boreham, Chelmsford, Essex CM3 3DE, **318**

Shapira, Aithan, 9 Cottage Street, Lexington, MA 2420, United States, **834**

Shapiro, Anna, 83 Candlemakers, 112 York Road, London SW11 3RS, **264**

SHAW, Tim, RA, Chyglidden, Higher Spargo Farm, Mabe, Nr. Penryn, Cornwall TR10 9JQ, **784, 787, 793, 888**

SHAWCROSS, Conrad, RA, Courtesy of the artist and Victoria Miro, London / Venice, **832**

Sherman, Kate, 4 Clayton Road, Ditchling, East Sussex BN6 8UY, **259**

Shih, Yimiao, 8 Golders Green Crescent, London NW11 8LE, **746**

Shinki, Tomoyuki, Everything Ltd, 3 Accurist House, 44 Baker Street, London W1U 7AL, **862**

Shiomi, Nana, 96A Greenvale Road, London SE9 1PF, **1021, 1024**

SHONIBARE, Yinka, MBE RA, Shonibare Studio, Sunbury House, 1 Andrews Road, London E8 4QL, **1276**

Shoukry, David, 37 Freestone Way, Corsham, Wiltshire SN13 9EE, **171**

Shrigley, David, Courtesy of Stephen Friedman Gallery, 25-28 Old Burlington Street, London W1S 3AN, **1296, 1297, 1298, 1299, 1300, 1301, 1302, 1303, 1304, 1305, 1306, 1307, 1308, 1309, 1310, 1311, 1312, 1313, 1314, 1315**

Singh, Shivraj, 3 Ridgewood Grove, Ravenshead, Nottingham NG15 9EN, **441**

Siu, Helen, Flat 5, Nicholas Court, 967 Finchley Road, London NW11 7EY, **603**

Skeggs, Jean, Clifton House, 34 Vicarage Lane, Shrivenham, Wiltshire SN5 8DT, **1064**

Sleigh, Bronwen, 63 Earlspark Avenue, Newlands, Glasgow G43 2HE, **897, 1263**

SMITH, Bob and Roberta, OBE RA, 49 Rhodesia Road, London E11 4DF, **51, 170, 977, 985**

Smith, Brian, Blacksmiths Corner, The Street, Lower Layham, Ipswich, Suffolk IP7 5LZ, **365**

Smith, John, 164 Richmond Road, Dalston, London E8 3HN, **750**

SMITH, Kiki, HON RA, **1234**

Smith, Richard C., Everything Ltd, 3 Accurist House, 44 Baker Street, London W1U 7AL, **774, 799**

Snoddy, Stephen, 10 Clarence Road, Heaton Moor, Stockport SK4 4RJ, **1214**

Sofia, Violeta, 105 Shelbourne Road, London N17 9YL, **143**

Songtao, Zhang, Hidden Dragon Island, Limiao Road, No.6, Jiangxia Wuhan Hubei, Wuhan 430205, China, **1342**

Sophie Thomas & Louis Thompson, 79 Queen Elizabeth's Walk, London N16 5UG, **796**

Sorrell, Richard, Higher Hellangove Farm, Badgers Cross, Gulval, Penzance, Cornwall TR20 8XD, **295**

Sorrentino, Filomena, 96 Victoria Road, London NW6 6QA, **355**

Southall, Tim, 17 Brook Holloway, Wollescote, Stourbridge, West Midlands DY9 8XJ, **1096**

Spare, Richard, 72 Ravensbourne Park, London SE6 4XZ, **936**

Squire & Partners, The Department Store, 248 Ferndale Road, London SW9 8FR, **618**

Stanhope Gate Architecture, 5 St James's Square, London SW1Y 4JU, **569**

Steen, Laurie, Higher Yellowford, Thorverton, Exeter, Devon EX5 5JR, **896**

Stephenson, Luke, 47 Claude Road, London E13 0QQ, **1284**

Stephenson, Roger, Stephenson Studio, 3 Riverside Mews, 4 Commercial Street, Manchester M15 4RQ, **605**, **608**

Stephenson, Simon, 44 Mulgrave Road, London NW10 1BT, **423**

Stevens, Calum, 25 Regent Park Terrace, Leeds LS6 2AX, **794**

Stewart, Alan, The Knapps, Barton Lane, Berrynarbor, Ilfracombe, Devon EX34 9SU, **440**

Stewart-Clark, Zarina, Squirrels Hall, Stubbins Lane, Holton St Mary, Colchester, Suffolk CO6 7NT, **913**

STIBBON, Emma, RA, 30 Islington Road, Bristol BS3 1QB, **890**, **891**, **892**, **894**, **895**, **1083**

Stockmarr, Alison, Dockside, 30 Walter Radcliffe Road, Wivenhoe, Colchester, Essex CO7 9FF, **1127**

Stubbs, Una, c/o Rebecca Blond, 69A Kings Road, London SW3 4NX, **363**

Studio DA, Unit 16, 5 Durham Yard, Teesdale Street, London E2 6QF, **531**

Studio Egret West, 3 Brewhouse Yard, London EC1V 4JQ, **510**, **577**

Studio 8 Architects, 95 Greencroft Gardens, London NW6 3PG, **521**

Summers, Jennifer, 67 Brackenbury Road, London N2 0SS, **14**

Sunderland, Paul, 24 Cheviot Drive, Bulwell, Nottingham NG6 7FH, **134**

SUTTON, Philip, RA, Harbour Cottage, Harbour House, George Street, West Bay, Bridport, Dorset DT6 4EY, **239**, **246**, **280**, **443**

Swan, Anselmo, 101-2130 York Avenue, Vancouver, V6K 1C3, Canada **1086**

Swayne, Geraldine, Flat 2, 2 Pevensey Road, St Leonards-on-Sea, East Sussex TN38 0JZ, **448**

Szczotka, Agnieszka, Burlington House, Piccadilly, London
   W1J 0BD, **20**

U

Udall, Laurence, 4 Godolphin Drive, Marazion, Penzance,
Cornwall TR17 0EP, **97**

Uglow, Geoff, Highermead, Egloskerry, Launceston, Cornwall
PL15 8RU, **860**

Underdown, Cynthia, Otterdale, Gittisham, Honiton, Devon
EX14 3AW, **1285**

Unga (Broken Fingaz), Flat 316, 419 Wick Lane, London E3 2PX,
344, 345

Unsworth, Jim, East Lodge, Syston Park, Grantham NG32 2DA, **844**

V

Vasconcelos, Joana, Atelier Joana Vasconcelos, Edifício Gonçalves
Zarco, Rua da Cintura do Porto de Lisboa, Doca de Alcântara
Norte, 1350-352 Lisbon, Portugal, **49**

Verity, Charlotte, 8 Love Walk, London SE5 8AD, **1055, 1058**

Vinyl, Kosmo, 407 Amsterdam Avenue, New York, NY 10024,
United States **322**

VIOLA, Bill, HON RA, Courtesy of Blain|Southern, 4 Hanover
Square, London W1S 1BP, **764**

Vollmer, Sheila, 35 Upper Tulse Hill, London SW2 2SG, **843**

W

Wade, Luke, 6 The Manor, Banbury Road, Moreton Pinkney,
Northamptonshire N11 3SJ, **166**

Wagstaff, Lee, 145A The Broadway, Thorpe Bay, Southend-on-Sea,
Essex SS1 3EX, **358**

Wagstaff, Lizzie, 15 Turner Street, Bollington, Macclesfield
SK10 5QH, **432**

Wake, Sophie, 10 Walpole Road, Brighton, East Sussex BN2 0EA, **72**

Walker, Katie, Millmead Studios, Coombelands Lane, Pulborough,
West Sussex RH20 1AG, **845**

Wallace, Douglas, 8 Printers Mews, London E3 5NZ, **391, 392**

Wallinger, Mark, Courtesy of Hauser & Wirth, 23 Savile Row,
London W1S 2ET, **766**

Wallis, Sheila, B3 Peabody Buildings, Duchy Street, London
SE1 8AQ, **138**

Warby, Jess, Flat 37, Grenier Apartments, 18 Gervase Street, London
SE15 2RS, **93**

Ward, Cynthia, 9 Ebor Manor, The Garth, Keyingham, East
Yorkshire HU12 9SN, **155**

Ward, Lucy, 110A Shooters Hill Road, London SE3 8RL, **1130**

Ward, Jane, 66 Mayall Road, London SE24 0PJ, **1257**

Ward-Raatikainen, Caroline, Vaalantie 22, Turku 20750, Finland,
1150

Warnants, Ceal, 24 Green Lane, London W7 2PB, **1173**

Watt, Laina, 25 Priory Street, Lewes, East Sussex BN7 1HH, **1336**

Waugh Thistleton Architects, 77 Leonard Street, London EC2A 4QS, **598**

Wedderburn, Georgina, 38 Tower Street, Winchester, Hampshire SO23 8TA, **52**

Welch, Jane, 25 Brooklands Avenue, London SW19 8EP, **1339**

Wells, Robert E., 2 Ruskin Road, Eastbourne, East Sussex BN20 9AY, **452**

Wentworth, Richard, Courtesy the artist and Peter Freeman, Inc., New York / Paris, **754**, Courtesy the Artist and Lisson Gallery, **761**

Westerhof, Tisna, 44 Musgrove Road, London SE14 5PW, **258**

Westmancoat, Deborah, Meadowside, Meadowside Close, Bishops Hull, Taunton, Somerset TA1 5DX, **962**

Wetherell, Imogen, 8 Highworth Avenue, Cambridge CB4 2BG, **263**

Whadcock, Ian, 113 Prestbury Road, Macclesfield SK10 3BU, **1105**

Wheatley, Jenny, Bristol House, Portloe, Truro, Cornwall TR2 5RG, **21**

Whiles, Annie, 48 The Keep, London SE3 0AF, **397, 795**

WHISHAW, Anthony, RA, 7a Albert Place, Victoria Road, London W8 5PD, **63, 70, 197, 858**

White, Peter, c/o Bethlem Gallery, Bethlem Royal Hospital, Monks Orchard Road, Beckenham, Kent BR3 3BX, **46, 244**

White, Fiona, 108 Heath Road, Pretty Beach, New South Wales 2257, Australia **340, 442**

Widener, George, Everything Ltd, 3 Accurist House, 44 Baker street, London W1U 7AL, **250**

Widjaja, Sudjadi, 1 Buckthorn House, Longlands Road, Sidcup, Kent DA15 7NA, **309**

Wiggin, Amy, Flat B, 89 Glyn Road, London E5 0JA, **949**

Wilde, Emma, 3 Bradwell Road, New Bradwell, Milton Keynes MK13 0EJ, **1175**

WILDING, Prof. Alison, RA, Courtesy of Karsten Schubert, 46 Lexington Street, London W1F 0LP, **721, 722, 723, 725**

Wilhide Justin, Carol, Flat 2, 7 Seymour Road, London N3 2NG, **1073**

WILKINSON, Chris, OBE RA, WilkinsonEyre, 33 Bowling Green Lane, London EC1R 0BJ, **657, 668**

Williams, Anthony, 1 Forres Avenue, Sheffield S10 1WG, **386**

Williams, Dan, 22 Walford Road, London N16 8ED, **173, 189**

Williams, Emrys, First Floor Flat, 10 Whitehall Road, Rhos-on-Sea LL28 4HW, **126**

Williams, Lucy, Flat 6, St Aubyns, 61 Snaresbrook Road, London E11 1PQ, **77**

Williams, Stanton, Crystal Wharf, 36 Graham Street, London N1 8GJ, **540, 543, 638**

Williams, Susan, Harford Cottages, 24 The Street, Wrecclesham, Farnham, Surrey GU10 4PR, **364**

Williams, Terry, Everything Ltd, 3 Accurist House, 44 Baker Street, London W1U 7AL, **778**

Williams Griffiths Architects, The Cooperage, 91 Brick Lane, London E1 6QL, **530**

WILSON, Jane & Louise, RA, **1258**

Wilson, Jess, c/o Jealous Gallery, 53 Curtain Road, London EC2A 3PT, **141**

Wilson, Karen, 40 Southdale Road, Wavertree, Liverpool L15 4HZ, **188**

Wilson, Kate, 7 Hotham Road, London SW19 1BS, **91**

Wilson, Matthew, 50a Loup Road, Moneymore, Magherafelt, Londonderry BT45 7SS, **375**

WILSON, Richard, RA, 44 Banyard Road, London SE16 2YA, **713, 714, 717, 1241**

Wilson, Sharon, Allendale Cottage, Bucks Hill, Kings Langley, Hertfordshire WD4 9AP, **427**

Wilson, Susan, 16 Balliol Road, London W10 6LX, **38**

Winstanley, Paul, Courtesy of Alan Cristea Gallery, 43 Pall Mall, London SW1Y 5JG, **1275**

Winston, Willow, Unit 17, Excelsior Works, Rollins Street, London SE15 1EP, **733**

Wix, Katy, 1 Coach House Mews, London SE23 3NT, **60**

Wood, Wilfrid, 56 Paragon Road, London E9 6NN, **1328**

WOODROW, Bill, RA, Studio North, Fryern Court Road, Burgate, Hampshire SP6 1NF, **684, 685, 686, 701**

Woods, Clare, Courtesy of Alan Cristea Gallery, 43 Pall Mall, London SW1Y 5JG, **976**

Woods, Richard, 27 Coate Street, London E2 9AG, **698, 699**

WRAGG, John, RA, 6 Castle Lane, Devizes, Wiltshire SN10 1HJ, **58, 271, 873, 878**

Wright & Wright Architects, 89-91 Bayham Street, London NW1 0AG, **636**

Wright, Stuart Pearson, Mettingham Castle, Castle Road, Mettingham, Bungay, Suffolk NR35 1TH, **184**

WYLIE, Rose, RA, 94 Teesdale Street, London E2 6PU, **123**

Original Prints Glossary

An original print is an artwork which the artist intended as a print (rather than being a reproduction of another work). There are three main methods of printing: relief, intaglio and planographic. These techniques can also be combined within a single print.

Relief printing

In relief printing, the areas around the image are cut away, leaving the image raised on the block. The raised areas are inked and the image is transferred onto paper by press or hand, using the back of a wooden spoon or a tool called a baren. Three common methods of relief printing are linocut, woodcut and wood engraving.
Linocut The areas around the image are cut into a sheet of linoleum, which is soft and relatively easy to carve.
Woodcut The areas around the image are cut into a wooden block cut across the grain – usually a soft wood such as pear or beech.
Wood engraving The areas around the image are cut into a harder wooden block, allowing for greater detail than a woodcut. The grain pattern is less visible in the finished print than in a woodcut.

Intaglio printing

In intaglio printing, the image itself is cut into the plate or block. When the plate or block is inked, the cut lines hold the ink, allowing the image to be transferred. Common methods of intaglio printing include engraving, etching, drypoint and mezzotint.
Engraving The image is scratched into a metal plate (usually copper), using a sharp tool called a burin.
Etching A wax covering is added to the plate and the image is drawn into the wax. The plate is then 'bitten' in acid, so the lines in the wax are transferred to the plate.
Softground etching The image is drawn on a piece of paper placed on top of a wax-covered plate. The plate is then bitten as above.
Drypoint The image is scratched onto a plate using a sharp needle. The resulting burr creates a fuzzy line once printed.
Mezzotint A tool called a rocker is used to give the entire plate a rough surface, which will hold the ink. The artist then introduces lighter tones to create the image on the plate.

Planographic printing

Unlike the more traditional relief and intaglio processes, planographic prints do not involve cutting into a block or plate. Planographic processes include lithograph, screenprint, monotype, and photomechanical and digital processes.
Lithograph The image is drawn onto a 'lithographic stone' using a greasy crayon. The grease repels water-based ink, so only the uncovered areas are printed.
Screenprint Ink is pushed through a stretched fabric (usually silk) using a tool called a squeegee. This process

is repeated using stencils to create the image.

Monotype Paint or ink is applied directly to a plate, and then transferred to paper. As such, there's only one copy.

Photomechanical The plate is prepared for printing using photography. The most common method is photogravure, which uses a light-sensitive gelatin tissue that allows a film positive to be transferred to a copper plate.

Digital A general term for prints where digital technology is used in the creation of an image or its printing. Methods of printing include inkjet and giclée and new methods are still being invented.

Other useful terms	

Aquatint A variant of intaglio printing. Tonal areas are added to the plate using rosin or asphalt, which is then bitten in acid to create texture.

Burr Ridges of metal which have been displaced when a plate is engraved. In drypoint, the burr creates the fuzzy effect.

Blind embossing A plate is printed without being inked, leaving a imprint on the paper.

Carborundum A variant of intaglio printing. The surface of the plate is built up using carborundum grit, which holds the ink and creates rich, dense tones.

Chine-collé Thin paper applied to the image during the printing process to add areas of colour.

Collagraph The plate is built up with materials such as card or fabric before being inked and printed in the intaglio method.

Counterprint This is created by passing a print, usually an etching, through the press a second time. This reverses the image and is useful when text is included.

C-type A digital or photographic print on high-quality paper.

Deckle edge The rough edge of handmade paper.

Edition The number of impressions of the print that will be made. A print's individual number is usually written on each impression e.g. 1/25.

Hand-colouring Colour, usually watercolour, which is applied to the image by hand after printing.

Impression Each print in an edition; a copy

Letterpress A relief-printing process historically used to reproduce text using block letters.

Matrix The general term for the surface (block, plate or stone) on which the image is produced.

Monoprint A unique print produced by making additions to a basic image, or by printing it in different colours.

Open bite etching An intaglio method where the plate is brushed directly with acid, to create tonal areas.

Proofs A number of prints that are kept apart from the official print run. These include trial proofs, working proofs, proofs kept back for the artist or the printer, and other prints that are not for sale.

State Each time an artist makes an alteration to a plate after it is first printed, this forms a new state.

Sugarlift A form of aquatint which uses a sugar solution

Stipple engraving A sharp point is used to create a mass of dots rather than lines of regular engraving.

Supporting the Royal Academy

The Royal Academy of Arts receives no revenue funding from government and is entirely reliant on self-generated income and charitable support.

Registered Charity No. 1125383

Friends of the Royal Academy

Become a Friend of the RA to enjoy free entry to all our world-class exhibitions with a family guest, priority booking to all RA events, an art-filled members' room, RA Magazine delivered to your door and much more.

Buy today at the Friends Desk or call 020 7300 8090. Find out more at roy.ac/friends

Donating to the Royal Academy and the Royal Academy Schools

Donations from individuals and charitable trusts enable the Royal Academy to support educational projects, extend the reach of the Learning Department and conserve the Royal Academy's Permanent Collection. For the young artists studying in the Royal Academy Schools, charitable support provides scholarships and bursaries so that they can live and study in London. For information on how to donate charitably, please contact Joanna Davidson at joanna.davidson@royalacademy.org.uk or Navasha Wray at navasha.wray@royalacademy.org.uk.

The Royal Academy Development Trust
Registered Charity No. 1067270

The Royal Academy Development Trust was founded in 1981 to receive, invest and disburse funds given in support of the Royal Academy of Arts. Since then the Trust has raised a significant endowment fund, the income from which helps to finance the Academy's charitable activities and capital projects including the Sackler Wing of Galleries, the Keeper's House and Burlington Gardens. For further information, please contact the Development Trust Office on 020 7300 5930 or email Charlotte Masters at charlotte.masters@royalacademy.org.uk.

Become a Patron

It was the support of a patron, George III, that enabled a small group of artists and architects to found the Royal Academy in 1768. While much has changed, we still rely on our Patrons and as a unique, artist-led organisation we offer them unrivalled opportunities to engage with art and artists.

For more information about becoming a Patron of the Royal Academy, please contact the Patrons Office on patrons@royalacademy.org.uk or 020 7300 5885, or visit www.royalacademy.org.uk/patrons.

Including a gift to the Royal Academy in your will

By including a gift to the Royal Academy in your will, you can help to protect all that we stand for, and ensure that we are there as a voice for art and for artists, whatever the future may hold.

A gift can be a sum of money, a specific item or a share of what is left after you have provided for your family and friends. Any gift, regardless of the size, can have an impact, and will allow art lovers to enjoy the Royal Academy in the years to come.

For more information please contact Frances Griffiths on 020 7300 5677, or email legacies@royalacademy.org.uk.

Corporate opportunities

For 250 years, the Royal Academy has remained both independent and self-supporting, receiving no government funding for its exhibitions or education programmes.

The RA has led the fields of arts sponsorship, corporate membership and corporate entertaining for over 30 years. Together, these aspects make a significant financial contribution, allowing us to continue making, exhibiting and debating art.

Since 1979 the RA has worked with over 200 sponsors in a range of areas, including exhibitions, education, fundraising events and the Royal Academy Schools. The team also looks after over 70 Corporate Members who enjoy numerous benefits for their staff, clients and community partners.

Sponsorship and Corporate Membership can offer companies:
- Priority booking of and exclusive entertaining in the suite of eighteenth-century John Madejski Fine Rooms and the brand-new RA Collection Gallery for business presentations, breakfasts or dinners combined with private views of exhibitions
- Exclusive hires of The Benjamin West Lecture Theatre for Corporate Founding Benefactors, a bolt-on to corporate membership
- Comprehensive crediting on all publicity material and involvement with press and promotions campaigns (sponsorship only)
- Invitations to prestigious Royal Academy corporate and social events
- Special passes for unlimited entry to all Royal Academy exhibitions
- Free entry for employees; behind-the-scenes tours; lectures and workshops for staff and their families
- Regular monitoring and evaluation
- A dedicated team of experienced staff to manage every aspect of sponsorship, corporate membership and corporate entertaining

For information about Corporate Membership and Sponsorship, please contact Stefanie Woodford on 020 7300 5936, or email stefanie.woodford@royalacademy.org.uk.

AGBI

Registered Charity No. 212667

Artists' General Benevolent Institution
Burlington House, Piccadilly, London W1J 0BB

Patron: HRH The Prince of Wales

Founded in 1814 by J. M. W. Turner, the AGBI provides help to professional artists and their dependants in time of trouble.

Funds are always needed and donations of any amount are gratefully received and acknowledged. Cheques should be sent to the Secretary at the above address.

Contact: 020 7734 1193   www.agbi.co.uk

Royal Academy Schools

The Royal Academy Schools is an independent school of art that offers a three-year, full-time postgraduate programme in fine art. The RA Schools has been an integral part of the Royal Academy of Arts since its foundation in 1768. A key principle of the RA Schools is that our programme is free of charge to any applicant offered a place.

The RA Schools thrives on the ability, commitment and intellectual inquiry of our students. With a maximum of 51 students, we are able to tailor our programme to the specific needs of each student, offering time and space to reflect and make. The comparatively small size of the RA Schools also allows us to be in a constant state of evolution, inflected by the contribution and experience of our participants.

Discussion and debate is fuelled by a variety of lectures, artist talks, group critiques and tutorials given by leading contemporary artists, Royal Academicians, critics, writers and theorists. Recent visitors have included Nick Fox Weber, Alison Katz, Siobhan Davies, Samara Scott, Enrico David and Harold Offeh and Royal Academicians Chantal Joffe, David Remfry, Vanessa Jackson and Cathie Pilkington.

Although the Royal Academy Schools are steeped in the atmosphere of history and tradition, we are a school of contemporary art. Graduates of RA Schools include J. M. W. Turner RA, William Blake and John Everett Millais PRA, all the way to more recent graduates such as Turner Prize nominee Lynette Yiadom-Boakye, Eddie Peake, Catherine Story and Matthew Darbyshire.

Published by RA Publications
Royal Academy of Arts
Piccadilly
London W1J 0BD

Compiled by Arzu Altin, Sinta Berry,
Catherine Coates, Bronte Earl,
Katherine Oliver, Paul Sirr and
Victoria Wells

Designed by Adam Brown_01.02
Production by Abbie Coppard, Rosie Hore and
    Luke Hoyland
Printed by Latimer Trend and Company Ltd

On the cover:
Michael Landy RA
Closing Down Sale
Mixed media and audio
H 165 cm

Architectural credits
523 Model by TaylorMade Model Makers
531 Design by Ryan McStay, model by James O'Brien and Joseph Van der Steen
553 Drawing by Emma Macey-Brown
561 Measured and drawn by Thomas Pearson
572, 669 Model by Azur-MGM
581 Model by Henry Milner
586 Model by Jonny Allams
590, 606 Model by A Models
609 Model by Scales&Models Ltd
611 Model by Marianne Weineck
613 Made by John Desmond Ltd
618 Model by The Modelshop team at Squire and Partners
625 Model by Danny Steadman
632 Model by Millennium Models. Photography by Simon Kennedy
652 Model developed by Hawkins\Brown in collaboration with School 21 pupils (Year 9)
    during The Big Draw Festival. Photography by Jack Hobhouse
653 Model by Scales&Models Ltd and Hobs Studio
654 Model by Andrew Ingham Associates. Photography by Nick Wood (image 1)
    and Grant Smith (image 2 and 3)
657, 668 Model by Wilkinson Eyre Model Making Workshop
661 Model by Tobias Klein
671 Model by RJ Models (Asia)
676 Model by PLP Modelmakers